# Claim

www.que

MW00779614

## Like our Facebook page
@QuestionsAboutMe

## Follow us on Instagram
@QuestionsAboutMe_Official

## Questions & Customer Service
hello@questionsaboutme.com

3000 Would You Rather Questions About Me

by Questions About Me™

**www.questionsaboutme.com**

# Introduction

Communication is key for meaningful relationships, but we often rely on small talk and dull exchanges without truly engaging others in deep conversation.

*3000 Would You Rather Questions About Me* is a tool to help spark engaging discussions and thoughts. You can use *3000 Would You Rather Questions About Me* to unlock endless conversational possibilities with someone you've known for years or someone you've recently met.

Enjoy learning more about yourself and foster conversation and engagement with others.

Ask yourself these dilemma-style questions or use them as conversation prompts with family and friends—even strangers!—to cultivate meaningful and fun discussions. These thought-provoking dilemmas will help you communicate and connect in an easy and entertaining way.

We've intentionally made the questions random so they're spontaneous. The dilemmas have been created for adults, but they're suitable for children as young as nine years old—we've included some extra easy questions for younger audiences.

Our *Questions About Me* series is for everyone—there's no adult content and the questions are free from political affiliation and religious preference.

## How to Use this Book

» You must choose an answer! The dilemmas will make you think and force you to make a choice.

» Going deeper with your answers by explaining your logic will lead to rewarding explorations and discussions.

» Don't be afraid to go off-topic. The wide range of intriguing scenarios will result in interesting conversations, lively discussions, and endless laughs!

» The format of this book is flexible and the questions can be tackled any way you like. You can skip around and answer questions, or you can start at the beginning and work through them in order.

» The writing space is purposely limited so you can use this book as a tool in a variety of ways—ask the questions out loud, fill in your responses, or answer the questions in your journal.

» Put down your phone, switch off the TV, and declare the time you spend answering these questions a no-judgment zone.

» Remember, there are no correct or incorrect answers. Allow yourself to be vulnerable and don't hold back with your responses.

You can enjoy our *Questions About Me* series on your own, one-on-one, or in a group setting.

# Yourself

- » Use as a guided journal, or question-a-day journal, for writing prompts or for creative inspiration.
- » Complete the questions as a mindfulness activity for self-reflection, personal growth, and better self-understanding.
- » Give a completed book to someone special as a keepsake.
- » Offer it as a unique and thoughtful gift to friends, family, a significant other, or yourself.

# One-on-one

- » Take turns asking questions with your significant other. Strengthen your relationship and bond with your partner by learning more about each other. (You could also get your partner to answer the questions as if they were you.)
- » Deepen your knowledge of those closest to you. Discover new things information about your kids, parents, siblings, and close friends with questions you never thought to ask.

# Group discussions

- » Stir up fun conversations at gatherings with family or friends at the dinner table, family events, or as a holiday activity.
- » Download the book and use while traveling.
- » Level up your conversation skills at networking events, team-building games, business trips, ice-breaker activities, job interviews, or therapy sessions.

The most important thing to know about using this book is: **There is no wrong way to use this book.** What's important is that you have fun.

No matter how you choose to use this book, enjoy using our *Questions About Me* series in any context or social situation to ignite meaningful connections and conversations.

01    WYR lose an arm or a leg?

02    WYR be too hot or too cold?

03    WYR Shrek and Donkey or Shaggy and Scooby-Doo were your house guests?

04    WYR win an Oscar or a Grammy?

05    WYR live in a world where nothing is square or one where nothing is round?

06    WYR be caught in an earthquake or a tornado?

07    WYR give up chocolate or give up cheese?

08    WYR be the size of a giraffe or the size of an ant for the day?

09    WYR hang out with King Arthur or Robin Hood?

10    WYR have a treehouse or an underground bunker?

11    WYR eat your favorite food every day or find a $5 bill under your pillow every morning?

12    WYR be able to swim like a fish or climb like a gecko?

13    WYR all your clothes had to be fastened with buttons or with zippers?

14    WYR reduce or recycle?

15    WYR have hiccups or a persistent cough for the day?

16    WYR be a world-class tap dancer or a world-class line dancer?

17    WYR take the stairs or use the elevator?

18    WYR cook a meal for six or wash the dishes after a meal for six?

19    WYR wear all stripes or wear all spots?

20    WYR shave off your hair or shave off your eyebrows?

21    WYR never eat red-colored food or never eat green-colored food again?

22    WYR never cut your fingernails or never cut your toenails again?

23    WYR be allergic to cola or coffee?

24    WYR receive $100 per day for life or receive one lump sum of $1 million?

25    WYR high five or fist bump?

26    WYR play a game of Scrabble or a game of Twister?

27    WYR have fur or feathers?

28    WYR be able to take a "Chance" card or a "Community Chest" card for real?

29    WYR visit the moon or the bottom of the deepest ocean?

30    WYR read a book or an eBook?

31    WYR have strawberries without cream or fries without ketchup?

32    WYR cozy up around a log fire or chill out around a pool?

33    WYR always be twenty minutes early or always be ten minutes late?

34    WYR have the go-ahead to get to the front of any line or always have traffic lights go green as you approach?

35    WYR give up soda or fried food?

36    WYR sit in the very front row or the very back row in a cinema?

37    WYR be a boy named Sue or a girl named Hank?

38    WYR live on a houseboat or in a motorhome?

39    WYR have a real or a fake Christmas tree?

40    WYR know everything there is to know or have access to the resources to research everything?

41    WYR have one lifelong friend or lots of short-term friends?

42    WYR eat hummus or refried beans?

43    WYR have tea with Sir Paul McCartney or Sir David Attenborough?

44    WYR drive a car or ride a motorbike?

45   WYR build a snowman or build a sandcastle?

46   WYR camp in a tent or stay in a campervan?

47   WYR holiday by the beach or in the forest?

48   WYR find the key to a secret door or the key to a secret box?

49   WYR have a grandfather clock or a cuckoo clock?

50   WYR eat roadkill or carrion?

51   WYR be sponsored by Coca-Cola or by Pepsi?

52   WYR colonize the moon or Mars?

53   WYR come face to face with a vampire or a werewolf?

54   WYR eat M&M's or Skittles?

55   WYR do a sponsored parachute jump or a sponsored bungee jump?

56   WYR there were only cats or only dogs in the world?

57   WYR be able to fly like Superman or teleport like the *Star Trek Enterprise* crew?

58   WYR never wear shoes or never go barefoot?

59   WYR know how to hunt or know how to fish?

60   WYR eat a filled donut or a glazed donut?

61   WYR have an attic or a basement in your home?

62   WYR write on a blackboard or a whiteboard?

63   WYR only watch TV series or only watch movies?

64   WYR own a teddy bear or a doll?

65   WYR have an open-plan living space or separate rooms in your home?

66   WYR bring a T-Rex or a woolly mammoth back to life?

67   WYR be the penguin keeper or the polar bear keeper at a zoo?

68    WYR slur your words like you're drunk or only be able to speak like a baby?

69    WYR dress like a Roman soldier or talk like a pirate for a month?

70    WYR own a treehouse or an underground bunker?

71    WYR never drink coffee or never drink tea?

72    WYR holiday in the sun or holiday in the snow?

73    WYR eat peanut butter without jelly or jelly without peanut butter in a sandwich?

74    WYR have just a smartphone or just a laptop computer?

75    WYR forget how to read or forget how to write?

76    WYR live on the first floor of an apartment building or the top floor (not penthouse)?

77    WYR float like a butterfly or sting like a bee?

78    WYR have no heating or no air conditioning?

79    WYR end world poverty or find a cure for cancer?

80    WYR be fluent in three languages or be able to talk to animals?

81    WYR lose your right thumb or both big toes?

82    WYR be somewhere over the rainbow or somewhere down the crazy river?

83    WYR have hooves or claws?

84    WYR be a fly on the wall or a snake in the grass?

85    WYR visit Middle-earth or Narnia?

86    WYR be a cyclops or a three-eyed monster?

87    WYR have your hands double in size or your feet double in size?

88    WYR spend the day with Harry Potter or Frodo Baggins?

89    WYR have only pink-colored Starbursts or only yellow?

90    WYR burn your finger or your tongue?

91    WYR be a solid-rooted tree or a leaf in the breeze?

92    WYR have the speed of a cheetah or the strength of a gorilla?

93    WYR be a champion cheerleader for a team you don't like or a mediocre cheerleader for a team you love?

94    WYR take a risk or play it safe?

95    WYR survive a plane crash into a jungle or into a desert?

96    WYR give up your seat on a crowded train to an elderly gentleman or a heavily pregnant lady?

97    WYR have a hat stuck to your head or shoes stuck to your feet for twenty-four hours?

98    WYR be a fashion designer or a landscape designer?

99    WYR have no hot water in your home or no indoor toilet?

100   WYR love your job and get paid a little or hate your job and get paid a lot?

101   WYR never have a BBQ or never have a burger in a bun ever again?

102   WYR be woken up every hour for forty-eight hours or stay awake for twenty-four hours?

103   WYR be a rocking horse or a Slinky?

104   WYR be attacked by two angry geese or six angry Chihuahuas?

105   WYR be able to make your own clothes or grow your own food?

106   WYR go to a costume party dressed as a historical figure or a cartoon character?

107   WYR never see the sea again or never see green fields again?

108   WYR have to sing everything you say or repeat everything you say?

109   WYR wear your slippers to work or your work shoes to the beach?

110   WYR do a thousand-piece jigsaw wearing ski gloves or walk up ten flights of stairs wearing scuba diving fins?

111    WYR wing walk or BASE jump?

112    WYR be a pirate or a highwayman?

113    WYR run a hundred-yard race running backward or wearing a hundred-pound backpack?

114    WYR attempt the world record for the highest jump on a pogo stick or fastest time to eat a bowl of pasta?

115    WYR be a famous movie director or famous songwriter?

116    WYR be able to breathe underwater or see in the dark?

117    WYR have wine pour out of the kitchen faucet or marshmallows rain out of the sky?

118    WYR save the last tree on Earth or the last bee on Earth?

119    WYR never have another cold or never have to charge up your devices?

120    WYR be the boss or be the boss's chief advisor?

121    WYR the last page of your book was missing or the last five minutes of the movie you're watching?

122    WYR not be able to read the labels in a supermarket or not be able to read the menu in a restaurant?

123    WYR be a prince turned into a frog or a sleeping princess awaiting true love's kiss?

124    WYR be lost in an unfamiliar city or lost in a forest?

125    WYR be invisible or be able to read minds?

126    WYR have only touchscreen devices or only keyboard devices?

127    WYR be able to type superfast or read superfast?

128    WYR never be able to send another text message or unable to send another email?

129    WYR have a beak for a week or walk on all fours for a week?

130    WYR only be able to read books for the rest of your life or only be able to watch movies for the rest of your life?

131    WYR be the best musician in a little-known band or the weakest musician in a well-known band?

132    WYR have a celebrity chef for a week or a housekeeper for a month?

133    WYR circumnavigate the globe as a solo yachtsperson or in a hot air balloon?

134    WYR have unlimited fries or unlimited potato chips for life?

135    WYR only be able to watch movies on your smartphone or only be able to listen to music through earbuds?

136    WYR have a huge surprise party organized in your honor or have an unlimited budget to organize a party for someone else?

137    WYR win the Nobel Prize for Medicine or for Peace?

138    WYR be able to build your own home or have enough money to pay someone to build it for you?

139    WYR have permanent dandruff or a constantly runny nose?

140    WYR be as sly as a fox or as gentle as a lamb?

141    WYR be a genie in a bottle or a leprechaun at the end of a rainbow?

142    WYR a professional photographer took your picture or a professional stylist styled your hair?

143    WYR never have to work again or never have to pay bills again?

144    WYR play hide and seek in the dark or dodgeball in the dark?

145    WYR have the eye of the tiger or eyes like a hawk?

146    WYR be trapped in an elevator with music you hate on a loop or with a celebrity you hate?

147    WYR accidentally brush your teeth with soap or wash your hair with toilet cleaner?

148    WYR be able to bound like a gazelle or show off like a peacock?

149    WYR be put on a puréed food diet or a raw food diet?

150 WYR your eyes could see like a microscope or far into the distance like binoculars?

151 WYR go out in public wearing just your oldest, ugliest underwear or just fig leaves?

152 WYR be on a glass-bottomed boat or in a glass-roofed submarine?

153 WYR have nothing but bread to eat for a week or give up Facebook for two weeks?

154 WYR lose the money you made this year or the memories you made this year?

155 WYR travel the world for five years on a shoestring budget or stay in only one country for a year but live in luxury?

156 WYR hop like a kangaroo or walk sideways like a crab?

157 WYR give up all the money you earn in the next five years or give up the savings you have now?

158 WYR have a ball pit in your bedroom or a slide from your bedroom to the yard?

159 WYR be hypnotized to dance every time you said "yes" or sing every time you said "no"?

160 WYR have ninja-like stealth or gladiator-like strength?

161 WYR eat bacon-flavored ice cream or curry-flavored candy?

162 WYR eat one witchetty grub or sit in a container full of spiders for twenty minutes?

163 WYR have slow internet for the rest of your life or eat the same dinner for the rest of your life?

164 WYR eat dinner alone for a year or eat with a group of people you don't like for a year?

165 WYR bring back Elvis or Princess Diana?

166 WYR be all-knowing or invulnerable?

167 WYR have no washing machine or no shower in your home for a year?

**168** WYR be able to press a fast-forward button or a rewind button in your life?

**169** WYR only have access to YouTube or only have access to games on your device?

**170** WYR be the first or the last to know the world is ending?

**171** WYR crawl 200 yards across a floor of mousetraps or swim 200 yards through shark-infested waters?

**172** WYR your face aged ten years overnight or your body from the neck down aged fifteen years overnight?

**173** WYR win $10,000 or have your friend win $25,000?

**174** WYR have someone constantly finish your sentences or someone constantly interrupt your conversations?

**175** WYR an alarm sounded every time you said a curse word or every time you lied?

**176** WYR be able to run but have nowhere to hide or hide and have nowhere to run?

**177** WYR win an all-expenses-paid dream vacation or go on tour with your favorite band?

**178** WYR have your toes stepped on every day or your hair pulled every day?

**179** WYR be a *Star Wars* Stormtrooper or a *Lord of the Rings* Orc?

**180** WYR be trapped in a small space with 5,000 locusts for ten minutes or eat ten locusts in five minutes?

**181** WYR never be able to wear the latest fashion or never be able to change your hairstyle?

**182** WYR always have an itchy nose or have at least one pimple on your face?

**183** WYR have one job for the rest of your life or change jobs every two years?

**184** WYR become half-human, half-fly or half-human, half-spider?

**185** WYR be able to play every musical instrument or sing every song?

186  WYR split your pants in public or snort out a booger when you laugh in public?

187  WYR be a secret benefactor or a famous philanthropist?

188  WYR have a small pebble in your shoe or a dull ringing in your ears?

189  WYR wear shoes that turned you into an excellent dancer or shoes that gave you super running speed?

190  WYR collect something few people care about or be an expert in something few people want to know?

191  WYR dress like your parents or only watch the TV shows your parents watch?

192  WYR win the Tour de France or win a silver medal in the Olympics?

193  WYR find a fly in your soup or a worm in your apple?

194  WYR be accused of something you didn't do or have someone else take the credit for something you did do?

195  WYR be stuck in an elevator with a bragger or a moaner?

196  WYR be able to do only one magical spell well or do lots of spells with only a fifty percent chance of success?

197  WYR never sunbathe again or never sit by an open fire again?

198  WYR be mentored by Bill Gates or Oprah Winfrey?

199  WYR be known for being kind or for being someone no one should mess with?

200  WYR be jilted at the altar or be divorced?

201  WYR have been born a decade earlier or a decade later than you were?

202  WYR never get another haircut or get a different trainee stylist every time you get a haircut?

203  WYR wear dark glasses at night or be forbidden from leaving your house after dark?

204  WYR be a fearless adventurer or a mathematical genius?

205 WYR have crackers without cheese or cheese without pickles?

206 WYR be able to walk through walls or see through walls?

207 WYR capsize your canoe into piranha-filled water or parachute into hippo territory?

208 WYR only be able to travel on horseback or by rickshaw?

209 WYR squeeze someone else's pimple or have someone squeeze your pimple?

210 WYR have the cleanliness of your fridge or your oven inspected right now?

211 WYR wake up in the body of a famous historical figure or the body of a reality-TV celebrity?

212 WYR lose three teeth or lose internet connection for three months?

213 WYR wear wet socks every day for a month or wear mitts on your hands every day for a week?

214 WYR only be able to listen to songs by your least favorite singer or watch movies starring your least favorite actor?

215 WYR have a pet dog that could whistle or a pet cat that could beatbox?

216 WYR be rich with a low IQ or poor with a high IQ?

217 WYR be transported into *Super Mario World* or into a *Candy Crush* world?

218 WYR play checkers or chess?

219 WYR everyone laughed when you walk into a room or everyone cried?

220 WYR tell the truth, no matter what, or tell a lie to save a friend?

221 WYR have someone massage your feet every day or have someone cook a meal for you once a week?

222 WYR emigrate and never return to your homeland or never leave your homeland at all?

223    WYR yawn uncontrollably or have your feet tap uncontrollably every time you hear music?

224    WYR be remembered as a great prankster or a great team player in your schooldays?

225    WYR wake up with a face like a fish or a neck like a giraffe?

226    WYR someone you just met told you your fly was undone or a colleague told you that you have bad breath?

227    WYR have vampire-like fangs or werewolf-like eyes?

228    WYR be telepathic or have the power to heal with your hands?

229    WYR experience zero gravity or be able to dance on the ceiling?

230    WYR be G.I. Joe or Stretch Armstrong?

231    WYR spend a day in an enchanted forest or in a magical undersea world?

232    WYR eat in the Great Hall at Hogwarts or feast in Neverland with the Lost Boys?

233    WYR have ears bigger than your hands or arms longer than your legs?

234    WYR bring back an outdated fashion or a forgotten food from decades ago?

235    WYR make snap decisions using your heart or your head?

236    WYR walk the plank or be marooned on a desert island?

237    WYR be stuck in a Groundhog Day loop on your first day at work or on a first date?

238    WYR sing a duet with Frank Sinatra or do a dance routine with Laurel and Hardy?

239    WYR visit the Simpsons or the Addams Family?

240    WYR be a guest at a party without food or a party without music?

241    WYR have a secret admirer or secretly know the identity of your secret admirer?

242   WYR eat ten bananas every day or slip on a banana peel every day?

243   WYR survive for a week on dog food or a week on food thrown out by grocery stores?

244   WYR be raised by wolves or monkeys?

245   WYR have your arm in plaster for six weeks or be on a strict liquid-only diet for three weeks?

246   WYR be a robot that builds cars or a robot that performs surgical procedures?

247   WYR have been the first person to walk on the moon or be the first person to walk on Mars?

248   WYR be the captain of a cruise ship or the pilot of a jumbo jet?

249   WYR spend a day on the Starship Enterprise or the Millennium Falcon?

250   WYR be the bearer of bad news or receive bad news?

251   WYR be a world-renowned concert pianist or the keyboard player in a popular tribute band?

252   WYR meet a wolf dressed in sheep's clothing or have the wool pulled over your eyes?

253   WYR be the eighth dwarf in *Snow White* or the fourth member of *Alvin and the Chipmunks*?

254   WYR be known as a lone wolf or a crowd-pleaser?

255   WYR have six-pack abs or get a free six-pack of potato chips whenever you want one?

256   WYR sneeze six times on the hour every hour or wink six times on the hour?

257   WYR eat a whole jar of mayonnaise straight from the jar or drink one liter of beetroot juice in one sitting?

258   WYR be a wildflower in a woodland or a rare orchid in a pot?

259   WYR be stranded on a desert island with an optimistic self-help guru or a pessimistic doom merchant?

260 WYR have no sense of smell or smell the opposite of what everyone else smells?

261 WYR save the life of one distant relative or save the lives of five people you don't know?

262 WYR survive on uncooked pasta or raw eggs?

263 WYR be a party balloon or a party popper?

264 WYR be locked in a room with no source of light or locked in room with a bright light permanently on?

265 WYR be a box of firecrackers or a supercharged single firework?

266 WYR be once bitten, twice shy or be in for a penny, in for a pound?

267 WYR follow the way of the dragon or follow the yellow brick road?

268 WYR lose weight by sticking to the cabbage soup diet or by doing two high-intensity exercise sessions per day?

269 WYR be caught on CCTV scratching your butt or practicing your dance moves?

270 WYR get to work (school) on stilts or go shopping on the weekend on a hoppity hop?

271 WYR be able to clear traffic jams by clapping your hands or get instant takeout by snapping your fingers?

272 WYR be trapped in a romantic comedy with your enemies or trapped in a horror movie with your friends?

273 WYR have feet like a Hobbit or ears like Dobby the house-elf?

274 WYR sit in a bath of cold baked beans or get or get slimed for charity?

275 WYR be a soccer player's sock or a ski-jumper's glove?

276 WYR see the sun rise from Mount Fuji or see the sun go down in the Serengeti?

277 WYR fail your driving test six times or get dumped six times in a row?

278 WYR be able to swing through trees like Tarzan or talk to animals like Dr. Dolittle?

279 WYR be homeless or live alone with no family and friends?

280 WYR be able to walk on water or have diamonds on the soles of your shoes?

281 WYR die of starvation or sell one of your kidneys to buy food?

282 WYR be reincarnated as a beautiful butterfly with a short life or a stray dog living on the street?

283 WYR be a notorious baddie everyone loves to hate or an unsung hero?

284 WYR have no wrists or no ankles?

285 WYR music had never been invented or movies had never been invented?

286 WYR eat only your favorite meal for every meal or never eat your favorite meal again?

287 WYR wear clown shoes for a day or a clown wig and nose for three days?

288 WYR have only virtual-world video game adventures or have only real-world outdoor adventures?

289 WYR go on a cross-country road trip or a cross-country train trip?

290 WYR only comedy movies starring Chevy Chase were ever made or only action movies starring Arnold Schwarzenegger?

291 WYR spend a weekend in a relaxing spa retreat or in Las Vegas?

292 WYR be a famous athlete or a famous actor playing the role of a famous athlete in a movie?

293 WYR be an early riser or a night owl?

294 WYR only ever hang out with no more than five friends or only ever go to huge parties?

295 WYR be known as witty or wise?

296  WYR live in a world where you never had to work again or one where you never had to sleep again?

297  WYR be afraid of the dark or sunlight?

298  WYR be a deep-sea diver or a high diver?

299  WYR wear dirty clothes or torn clothes?

300  WYR receive $1,000 for kissing a stranger or $1 every time someone kisses you?

301  WYR go wilderness camping off the beaten track or go glamping in a popular tourist spot?

302  WYR your friends described you as someone who eats a lot or someone who sleeps a lot?

303  WYR always eat indoors or always eat outdoors?

304  WYR be an ordinary citizen in a utopian world or be a powerful leader in a dystopian world?

305  WYR be described as stern and stoic or frivolous and fun?

306  WYR be in a dull, long-lasting relationship or an exciting, short-lived relationship?

307  WYR wake up with teeth like a beaver or eyes like a lizard?

308  WYR be Goldilocks or Jiminy Cricket?

309  WYR be the runt of the litter or the black sheep of the family?

310  WYR survive by drinking the water in the toilet brush holder or eating frog spawn?

311  WYR never eat out or eat out once a week at a five-star restaurant for free with someone you don't like?

312  WYR relax by having a massage or by reading a magazine?

313  WYR that oranges were the only fruit you could eat or carrots were the only vegetable you could eat?

314  WYR be like someone else or stay as you are?

**315** WYR win the lottery or have everyone in your family (including you) live twice as long?

**316** WYR be stranded for an hour on a broken ski lift or a broken rollercoaster?

**317** WYR end all war or find a cure for all disease?

**318** WYR win a cash prize or a mystery prize of at least equal value?

**319** WYR work your way from rags to riches or win the lottery?

**320** WYR be an only child or the youngest of seven children?

**321** WYR have Captain America or Wolverine as a personal bodyguard?

**322** WYR swing on a star or carry moonbeams home in a jar?

**323** WYR go on a cruise with friends or stay at a luxury private island resort with family members?

**324** WYR only listen to music from the 1980s or only watch movies from the 1980s?

**325** WYR shoot lightning from your fingers or turn things to ice with your stare?

**326** WYR be a Guardian of the Galaxy or a Power Ranger?

**327** WYR have the Terminator or Magneto on your dodgeball team?

**328** WYR be able to wash your face like a cat or scratch behind your ears like a dog?

**329** WYR slither like a snake or hop like a frog?

**330** WYR noisy neighbors kept you awake or nosy neighbors watched your every move?

**331** WYR have shorter work hours each week or longer vacations each year?

**332** WYR communicate by smoke signals or by carrier pigeon?

**333** WYR work in a team or work alone?

**334** WYR live in a beach house or a mountain chalet?

335  WYR hear the bad news or the good news first?

336  WYR dress head to toe in tartan or in a paisley pattern?

337  WYR be your own boss or work for an awesome boss?

338  WYR have a pain in your neck or have a pain in your butt?

339  WYR be a wealthy person living in 1760 or be on an average income living in 1960?

340  WYR be trapped in an elevator with someone who picks and flicks or someone who farts incessantly?

341  WYR be a celebrity chef or have a personal chef?

342  WYR be in the crowd at a big sports game or at home watching the game live on TV?

343  WYR be the worm that turned or the fish that got away?

344  WYR invent an instant weight-loss plan that works or an anti-aging cream that works?

345  WYR stand out from the crowd or blend into the background?

346  WYR wear your underpants on the outside like Superman or wear a mask like the Lone Ranger?

347  WYR cut your hand off to escape death or abandon a friend in danger to escape death?

348  WYR have no say in what you eat or no say in what you watch on TV?

349  WYR be the nerd who cracks the code to save the world or the action hero who kills off the baddies?

350  WYR your flight was canceled or you lost your luggage?

351  WYR have a koala cling to your leg or a sloth hang around your neck?

352  WYR live next door to a rooster that crows at dawn or a dog that howls at midnight?

353  WYR eat hot yogurt or cold beef stew?

**354** WYR never know who your father is or discover your father is serving a life sentence in prison?

**355** WYR sprout feathers like a cockatoo on your head or have bumblebee-striped hair?

**356** WYR have a toothache or an earache for a week?

**357** WYR color within the lines or think outside the box?

**358** WYR wear a sleeping cat or a sleeping squirrel as a hat?

**359** WYR be the man in the moon or the cow that jumped over the moon?

**360** WYR be the shortest person on the basketball team or the tallest person on the "how many people in a Minivan" team?

**361** WYR be the star player in the losing team or on the subs bench in the winning team?

**362** WYR have too little time and so much to do or have too little to do and so much time?

**363** WYR be a good player in a televised sport or a champion player in a lesser-known sport?

**364** WYR be attracted to light like a moth or get sunburned when you sit under an electric light?

**365** WYR have a private pilot's license or be able to charter a private jet whenever you want?

**366** WYR time travel to meet a world leader of the past or a world leader fifty years into the future?

**367** WYR join a traveling circus or join the French Foreign Legion?

**368** WYR be the bee's knees or the cat's pajamas?

**369** WYR travel by dog sled or by horse and carriage?

**370** WYR your kettle played the national anthem when it boiled or the toilet played *The Simpsons*'s theme when flushed?

**371** WYR have an indoor job or an outdoor job?

**372** WYR try to leave a restaurant without paying or get pranked with a bucket of water when you go through a door?

**373** WYR have a cocktail named after you or a cologne named after you?

**374** WYR be the first person to step onto the rickety rope bridge or the last person in line for the lifeboat?

**375** WYR be famous and constantly hounded by paparazzi or famous and almost forgotten by the press?

**376** WYR shave your head or never brush your hair again?

**377** WYR upcycle old furniture or be minimalist with very little furniture?

**378** WYR be stranded in an airport for forty-eight hours or stuck at home for four days without power?

**379** WYR be in an arranged marriage or remain single for life?

**380** WYR be pulled from the crowd to sing at a country music festival or be a participant in a hypnotist's act?

**381** WYR babysit a crying baby or have a noisy teenage houseguest?

**382** WYR be the frosting on the cake or the jelly in the donut?

**383** WYR get dog poop on your shoe or sand in your eye?

**384** WYR be a Greyhound bus driver or a subway train driver?

**385** WYR meet the cast of *Friends* at Central Perk or the cast of *Cheers* at Cheers?

**386** WYR be a flea on a dog or a crocodile bird in a crocodile's mouth?

**387** WYR go speed dating or have a friend set you up on a blind date?

**388** WYR wear the same underpants or the same socks for two days?

**389** WYR be a ventriloquist's dummy or a puppet on a string?

**390** WYR slide down the banister or swing from the chandelier?

**391** WYR have a fairy godmother or have Santa Claus as your uncle?

392    WYR ride on the Polar Express or the Hogwarts Express?

393    WYR learn how to eat fire or learn how to ride a motorcycle wall of death?

394    WYR ride a unicorn or swim with a mermaid?

395    WYR be the pet sitter for 101 Dalmatians or the babysitter for the old woman who lived in a shoe?

396    WYR tiptoe through the tulips or walk on the wild side?

397    WYR be able to see through walls or listen in on conversations a block away?

398    WYR get yelled at by a stranger every day or buy a coffee for a stranger every day?

399    WYR get brain freeze every time you eat or bite your tongue every time you eat?

400    WYR swim with dolphins or soar with eagles?

401    WYR have an Elf on the Shelf or toilet roll on the shelf?

402    WYR try to walk up a slippery slope or climb a greasy pole?

403    WYR know the answer to every riddle or know how to order beer and pizza in every language?

404    WYR have a hairless cat or a hairless dog?

405    WYR be a salty dog or the cat that got the cream?

406    WYR have a real lightsaber or a real Excalibur?

407    WYR dress only in leisure wear or only in formal wear for the rest of your life?

408    WYR spend three weeks in prison or six weeks under house arrest?

409    WYR have a healing finger like E.T. or self-healing powers like Wolverine?

410    WYR get rid of Times New Roman font or Arial font?

411    WYR be able to redesign your body every day like the Sims or get designer clothes for free?

412   WYR have the highest number of followers on Twitter or on TikTok?

413   WYR your seat at a restaurant table was a little too low or a little too high?

414   WYR wash the cut on your hand in lemon juice and salt or get lemon juice in your eye?

415   WYR get punched by Mike Tyson or kicked by Bruce Lee?

416   WYR suffer from one long-term health condition or go through life believing you have every condition?

417   WYR have Cheetos dust on your fingers forever or the smell of onions on your fingers forever?

418   WYR never hit your funny bone again or never stub your toe again?

419   WYR have Batman's Batmobile or Iron Man's suit?

420   WYR hear Simon Cowell critique Gordon Ramsay's singing or Gordon Ramsay critique Simon Cowell's cooking?

421   WYR be the manager of a store with underperforming employees or be one of the underperforming employees?

422   WYR breathe fire like a dragon or rise from the flames like a phoenix?

423   WYR have Captain America's shield or Neptune's (Poseidon's) trident?

424   WYR go to Hogwarts School of Witchcraft and Wizardry or Xavier's School for Gifted Youngsters?

425   WYR have arms like an extended Mr. Tickle or arms like a T-Rex?

426   WYR be tickled for five minutes every day or be made to listen to one-liner jokes for ten minutes every day?

427   WYR be indestructible or invisible?

428   WYR spend an afternoon with Captain Hook or Darth Vader?

429   WYR have no thumbs or no fingers?

430 WYR slip on a banana peel and fall on your butt or step barefoot on a Lego brick?

431 WYR be a toy soldier or a toy car for a day?

432 WYR be Rick-rolled or be a famous internet troll?

433 WYR have hair like Rapunzel or wings like Tinkerbell?

434 WYR be a Jedi or a Minion?

435 WYR be a bull in a china shop or as timid as a mouse?

436 WYR have your face on the front cover of a magazine or your name on the front of a book?

437 WYR sharks could walk on land or lions could swim underwater?

438 WYR prove the existence of the Loch Ness Monster or leprechauns?

439 WYR have Bilbo Baggins's sword or Robin Hood's bow and arrow?

440 WYR be hugely famous for a few years in your lifetime or achieve fame after your death?

441 WYR have a real Millennium Falcon or a real time-traveling DeLorean?

442 WYR be able to control light switches or switch TV channels using your mind?

443 WYR only be able to speak to give orders or only be able to walk by marching?

444 WYR have a snot-and-earwax smoothie or a fish-gut-and-toe-cheese sandwich?

445 WYR be a volcano or a waterfall?

446 WYR have a good memory or be able to learn a new language easily?

447 WYR smell the aroma of freshly-baked bread or freshly-cut flowers?

448 WYR be able to talk to trees or interpret whale song?

**449**   WYR have no eyebrows or super-long nasal hair?

**450**   WYR eat a whole raw onion or drink a raw-egg shake?

**451**   WYR be a lion in captivity or a bear in the wild in hunting season?

**452**   WYR only be able to eat raw foods or only be able to eat canned foods?

**453**   WYR have an actual button for a nose or a clown's nose?

**454**   WYR be able to see in the dark like a cat or use echolocation like a bat?

**455**   WYR have a sniffly cold three times a year or a heavy cold once a year?

**456**   WYR be able to move things with your mind or read other people's minds?

**457**   WYR search for a needle in a haystack or go on a wild goose chase?

**458**   WYR be flavor of the month or an acquired taste?

**459**   WYR have wings like a griffin or a tail like a dragon?

**460**   WYR your milkshake was too warm or your coffee too cold?

**461**   WYR have no sense of humor or have no one ever laugh at your jokes?

**462**   WYR be a street artist or street musician?

**463**   WYR have multiple piercings on your face or a tattoo on your face?

**464**   WYR hear a bump in the night or hear a scratching sound in the night?

**465**   WYR have dandruff or have a bad hair day every other day?

**466**   WYR live in an old-fashioned windmill or an ancient castle with a moat?

**467**   WYR only be able to move around on a skateboard or on roller skates?

**468**   WYR never wear socks or always wear odd socks?

469  WYR have tennis elbow or housemaid's knee?

470  WYR never cry again or never dance again?

471  WYR have a film crew follow your every move for a week or have zero contact with anyone for a week?

472  WYR fly first class for free for a year or fly economy class for free for ten years?

473  WYR be able to pitch a baseball at 100 mph or ace a tennis serve at 150 mph?

474  WYR never be able to run again or never be able to sing again?

475  WYR spend one hour in a public library every day or two hours in a public swimming pool once a week?

476  WYR die surrounded by family at the age of 40 or outlive most of your family and die at the age of 104?

477  WYR have no eyelashes or no fingernails?

478  WYR be able to spin your head like an owl or change color like a chameleon?

479  WYR wake up on a raft in the middle of the ocean or on a blanket in the middle of a desert?

480  WYR have four arms and no legs or four legs and no arms?

481  WYR eat a snail a day or a giant centipede once a month?

482  WYR live in your dream house in your least favorite location or an ugly house in your favorite location?

483  WYR be covered in scales for two full days or be covered in fur from 6 pm to 6 am for a week?

484  WYR see no daylight for a month or be under nighttime curfew for a month?

485  WYR walk barefoot in a city or walk barefoot in a jungle?

486  WYR be below-average height or earn a below-average income?

487  WYR be a world-champion yodeler or a world-champion thumb wrestler?

488  WYR paint the outside of your house neon pink or share your house with a colony of bats?

489  WYR never eat freshly baked bread ever again or never drink freshly squeezed fruit juice ever again?

490  WYR go from riches to rags or from A-lister to nobody?

491  WYR get great grades at school without trying or be great at all sports without trying?

492  WYR eat toast without any spread or potato chips without flavoring?

493  WYR the wind was on your back when you cycled or you had clear roads when driving?

494  WYR have your hands tied behind your back or your ankles tied together?

495  WYR discover a dark family secret or have a skeleton in your closet revealed?

496  WYR it rained for forty days and forty nights or a gale-force wind blew for forty days and forty nights?

497  WYR have a personal chef or a personal maid?

498  WYR be a circus performer or a catwalk model?

499  WYR buy no new clothes for a year or have new clothes every day chosen for you by someone else?

500  WYR be the butt of a joke or be the last person to get the joke?

501  WYR be an Olympic archer or a skilled knife thrower?

502  WYR never have to blow your nose again or never have the hiccups ever again?

503  WYR wear shoes that pinch or underpants a size too small?

504  WYR be a record-breaker or a champion breakdancer?

505  WYR giant pandas were the size of penguins or Chihuahuas were the size of lions?

**506** WYR be in debt for $100,000 or never be able to earn more than $3,500 a month?

**507** WYR hang out with Puss in Boots or with Pinocchio?

**508** WYR your friend's worst habit was nail biting or lip smacking?

**509** WYR be a competitor in underwater hockey or extreme ironing?

**510** WYR live in a world without all things Disney or all things Hershey?

**511** WYR be a Lego mini-figure or a Buzz Lightyear doll?

**512** WYR be the worst singer or the worst dancer in a pop band?

**513** WYR not know where your next meal is coming from or not know where you're sleeping tonight?

**514** WYR hang out with Ed Sheeran or go on an adventure with Bear Grylls?

**515** WYR binge watch every *Harry Potter* movie or every *Looney Tunes* cartoon ever made?

**516** WYR know how to train your dragon or how to do the Expelliarmus spell?

**517** WYR wear a Christmas sweater all year round or listen to Christmas music every day?

**518** WYR be hugged by Paddington Bear or Winnie the Pooh?

**519** WYR have nonstop diarrhea for two days or vomit every morning for two weeks?

**520** WYR sleep fully clothed (including shoes) or sleep with a bright spotlight on you?

**521** WYR make horse hoof noises with coconut shells as you walk or wear squeaking clown shoes?

**522** WYR struggle to wake up every morning or struggle to get to sleep every night?

**523** WYR be joined by the neighborhood stray dogs when you go for a jog or by a group of jogging moms with strollers?

**524** WYR only get to change your clothes once a week or have a shower once a week?

**525** WYR everything left a bad taste in your mouth or everything had a bad smell?

**526** WYR never get another paper cut or never burn your tongue again?

**527** WYR be hungry or be tired?

**528** WYR be guaranteed never to fart in public or never say the wrong thing again?

**529** WYR have an awesome-looking car that can only reach 60 mph or a rust bucket that can reach 200 mph?

**530** WYR spend the day as Mario or Sonic?

**531** WYR have an amazing body and a plain face or a gorgeous face and a not-so-great body?

**532** WYR be trapped in a room full of party balloons and sharp-clawed kittens or a room full of toddlers with kazoos?

**533** WYR have a credit card with a $10,000 limit or $1,000 cash?

**534** WYR someone rained on your parade or be told you are a wet blanket?

**535** WYR be able to move like Mick Jagger or sing like Aretha Franklin?

**536** WYR get drive-thru meals for free or free amusement park entry for life?

**537** WYR never get another spam email or another spam phone call?

**538** WYR live in the middle of nowhere or live and work in the center of a busy metropolis?

**539** WYR rent a residence in three different cities or own one house in your hometown?

**540** WYR ride a rollercoaster or ride the waves?

**541** WYR look twenty-one years old physically or feel twenty-one years old mentally?

542 WYR be able to bounce on clouds or slide down a rainbow?

543 WYR be a black belt in karate or a tai chi master?

544 WYR be a one-hit wonder as a best-selling author or as the singer of a chart-topping novelty song?

545 WYR win a local talent contest or place third in a national contest?

546 WYR be a contestant on a TV game show or a reality TV survival show?

547 WYR be an inner-city cop or an inner-city high school teacher?

548 WYR meet Wyatt Earp or Abraham Lincoln?

549 WYR be able to snap your fingers and change your eye color or your hair color?

550 WYR be in the history books as a renowned scientist or a renowned artist?

551 WYR be a first-time parent at the age of eighteen or the age of forty?

552 WYR have blacksmithing skills or surgical skills?

553 WYR have too many friends or too few?

554 WYR sing in front of friends or in front of strangers?

555 WYR be friends with Willy Wonka or Sherlock Holmes?

556 WYR be the cat with the fiddle or the dish that ran away with the spoon?

557 WYR be a Jack-of-all-trades or a Jack-in-the-box toy?

558 WYR have retractable claws or razor-sharp teeth?

559 WYR accidentally shoot yourself in the foot or chop off a finger?

560 WYR always eat waffles for breakfast or always eat pizza for lunch?

561 WYR be very talented or extremely lucky?

562 WYR be the funniest person in your class at school or the smartest person in your workplace?

563 WYR live with messy but fun housemates or tidy but boring housemates?

564 WYR have a real-life *Star Trek* holodeck or a bowling alley in your home?

565 WYR have a mouth like a cat's butt or have your eyes switch places with your nipples?

566 WYR see a ghostly apparition or feel a presence in your bedroom at night?

567 WYR never be able to fully close your mouth or never fully open one eye?

568 WYR go surfing or surf the internet?

569 WYR have unlimited credit or endless battery charge on your phone?

570 WYR live without electricity for two days or live without hot food for a week?

571 WYR have cosmetic surgery to change your nose or change your teeth?

572 WYR your nose bled for fifteen minutes or you hiccupped for an hour?

573 WYR walk barefoot across a floor of broken glass or step barefoot on one upturned thumb tack?

574 WYR never swim in the sea again or never sled in the snow again?

575 WYR never be in another awkward silence or never fill out an application form ever again?

576 WYR have no air conditioning or no music in your car?

577 WYR share a toothbrush with a friend or borrow used underwear from a friend?

578 WYR literally have eyes in the back of your head or literally have lightning reflexes?

579 WYR be twice your weight or half your height?

580 WYR be given $10,000 today or $1 million in ten years' time?

581 WYR never get married or never have a best friend?

582 WYR be a farmer or a podiatrist?

583 WYR rescue the three-legged puppy or the one-eyed kitten from the animal shelter?

584 WYR have been a pioneer on a wagon train or a team member of the Apollo 11 moon mission?

585 WYR be the brightest star in the sky or the tallest mountain in the range?

586 WYR find your forgotten stash of candy or a forgotten box of old photographs?

587 WYR see the northern lights or a total eclipse of the sun?

588 WYR be able to change the ending of the last movie you saw or change the actors in the lead roles?

589 WYR find proof of alien life or find proof there's no other life in the universe?

590 WYR be quarantined for three months alone or with extended family members?

591 WYR have no toaster or no blender in your kitchen?

592 WYR be itchy or be cold?

593 WYR have an operatic singing voice or a raspy, rock singer voice?

594 WYR sleep sitting up or sleep lying down but unable to change position?

595 WYR have only spring and fall or only summer and winter?

596 WYR sing like a bird instead of talking or talk like Chewbacca?

597 WYR be a taxi driver in New York or an ice road trucker in Alaska?

598 WYR wake up to find your hair had fallen out or your teeth had fallen out?

599 WYR make the world's best bagels or the world's best pretzels?

**600**   WYR be the sharpest tool in the box or the cutest puppy in the litter?

**601**   WYR wear a swimsuit and sunscreen in Antarctica or a swimsuit and no sunscreen in the Sahara?

**602**   WYR sit in a room with 10,000 spiders or eat 100 spiders?

**603**   WYR be typecast as a rom-com sweetie or an evil villain?

**604**   WYR be the princess in "The Princess and the Pea" or one of the Twelve Dancing Princesses?

**605**   WYR be an @ symbol or an exclamation point?

**606**   WYR have super-strength by night or a photographic memory by day?

**607**   WYR be a tadpole or a chrysalis?

**608**   WYR meet the Gruffalo or the Lorax?

**609**   WYR have eggy burps or garlic breath?

**610**   WYR be Babe the sheep-pig or Stuart Little the mouse?

**611**   WYR be a Formula One driver or a Red Bull Air Race pilot?

**612**   WYR chop onions or have sticky fingers?

**613**   WYR have a feather tickle your nose or tickle your feet?

**614**   WYR be a sword swallower or a human cannonball?

**615**   WYR have a frantic Friday or a manic Monday?

**616**   WYR use 1960s slang or wear 1990s fashion?

**617**   WYR hand-stitch 1,000 sequins onto a gown or handwash your clothes for a week?

**618**   WYR be a dog that jumps through hoops of fire or a squirrel that crosses a tightrope?

**619**   WYR hang out at the Batcave under Wayne Manor or the Thunderbird secret base on Tracy Island?

**620**   WYR have reflective eyes or glow-in-the-dark hands?

621  WYR be in prison for a year or homeless for a year?

622  WYR have sweaty palms or sweaty armpits on a first date?

623  WYR never dance again or dance nonstop for forty-eight hours?

624  WYR have tunnel vision in color or clear vision in black and white only?

625  WYR be able to ride a unicycle or spin plates?

626  WYR never be in debt or never eat ice cream again?

627  WYR have an excellent poker face or wear your heart on your sleeve?

628  WYR find a dragon's treasure or a pirate's treasure?

629  WYR live in a world with giant earthworms or giant birds?

630  WYR have a car that never wears out or never have to pay for gas again?

631  WYR be chased by a clown or a billy goat?

632  WYR have no taste buds or be color blind?

633  WYR have to pee in public or have an unflattering picture of yourself posted on social media?

634  WYR be limited to 140 characters of text per day instead of talking or only be able to communicate using emojis?

635  WYR never see your face in a mirror again or never remember anyone's name other than your own?

636  WYR be without access to social media or to search engines?

637  WYR have free access to every circus for life or free access to every gym for a year?

638  WYR be an organ donor or donate your body to science?

639  WYR be stuck in an elevator with two grumpy people or one sweet person with two smelly dogs?

640  WYR snort like a pig when you laugh or bray like a donkey when you laugh?

641 WYR only age from the neck up or the neck down?

642 WYR be the Sandman or the Tooth Fairy?

643 WYR have the power to remove yourself from embarrassing situations or the power to move objects with your mind?

644 WYR hold an octopus or a jellyfish?

645 WYR be able to bring the pictures you draw to life or be able to step into the pictures in storybooks?

646 WYR be deaf in one ear or blind in one eye?

647 WYR be a banana smoothie or a banana muffin?

648 WYR be granted three wishes that can't include money or given $1 million a year for three years?

649 WYR have everyone laugh at you for farting or be the only one to laugh when someone else farts?

650 WYR wear a mohawk hairstyle for a month or clown makeup every day for a month?

651 WYR control gravity or control time?

652 WYR skip breakfast every day or eat breakfast cereal for lunch every day?

653 WYR be hopelessly underdressed or more than fashionably late for important events?

654 WYR *always feel* like someone is following you or actually *have* someone following you?

655 WYR go back in time and have VIP tickets to see Prince in concert or Freddie Mercury in concert?

656 WYR have a huge home with no yard or a tiny home with a huge yard?

657 WYR be able to shapeshift into other living things or into inanimate objects?

658 WYR be a James Bond villain or a Disney villain?

659 WYR never eat peanut butter again or never eat brownies again?

**660** WYR be able to switch your sense of smell on and off or switch your emotions on and off?

**661** WYR have an ugly phone with awesome features or an awesome-looking phone with only standard features?

**662** WYR choose cheesecake or fudge if only one could exist?

**663** WYR have your last phone conversation broadcast on national radio or your last thought appear in words over your head?

**664** WYR retake your driving test every year or retake high school tests every five years?

**665** WYR end animal testing or ban zoos?

**666** WYR play Dungeons and Dragons or Monopoly for a full day?

**667** WYR circus clown music ("Entry of the Gladiators") or *The Lone Ranger* theme (the *William Tell* Overture) played whenever you enter a room?

**668** WYR invent a solution to world pollution or world hunger?

**669** WYR save the last tree on Earth from destruction or save the Siberian tiger from extinction?

**670** WYR be able to charge your phone from your belly button or have a third eye in your fingertip?

**671** WYR both your feet were left feet or your hands were left hands?

**672** WYR be attacked by a giant snake or an angry piranha?

**673** WYR be a firefighter or a rescue helicopter pilot?

**674** WYR be part of a bobsled team or an acrobatic display team?

**675** WYR be able to join the Mad Hatter's tea party or a teddy bears' picnic?

**676** WYR hang out with the Pink Panther or the Black Panther?

**677** WYR sing the songs from *The Lion King* or *The Jungle Book*?

**678** WYR only be able to go to Justin Bieber concerts or Slipknot concerts?

679  WYR go to work in your party clothes or go to a party in your work clothes?

680  WYR be one of the Fab Four (Beatles) or one of the Fantastic Four (Marvel)?

681  WYR be able to move at *The Matrix*'s "bullet time" speed or *X-Men*'s Quicksilver speed at will?

682  WYR save a stranger's life by giving CPR or help a stranger give birth?

683  WYR sit in a bathtub of Nutella or maple syrup?

684  WYR get dressed in the dark or wear your clothes back to front?

685  WYR avoid black cats crossing your path or walking under ladders?

686  WYR work for a furniture removal company or a graffiti removal company?

687  WYR be Little Bo Peep or Miss Muffet?

688  WYR be able to magically lower the volume of crying babies in public places or traffic noise on the street?

689  WYR live in a mole hole or a bird's nest?

690  WYR go swimming with your socks on or wear socks with sandals?

691  WYR never get angry or never be envious?

692  WYR see a rat in your kitchen or a bat in your bedroom?

693  WYR poke yourself in the eye or bite your tongue?

694  WYR never get stuck in traffic again or never struggle to find a parking spot again?

695  WYR sleep in a doghouse or have a slobbery dog sleep in your bed?

696  WYR breathe like Darth Vader or talk like Mickey Mouse?

697  WYR be the Bionic Man or Bionic Bunny?

698  WYR eat a Milky Way bar deep-fried in batter or a chocolate-coated pizza?

**699** WYR work in Silicon Valley or Hollywood?

**700** WYR be a beekeeper or a bookkeeper?

**701** WYR spend a day in the life of *Downton Abbey* characters or *Outlander* characters?

**702** WYR have Raymond Babbitt's (*Rain Man*) savant abilities or David Copperfield's illusionist abilities?

**703** WYR change the ending to the story of *Beauty and the Beast* or "Little Red Riding Hood"?

**704** WYR be a horse and dog trainer or a Pokémon trainer?

**705** WYR have the powers of Tinkerbell in *Peter Pan* or Elsa in *Frozen*?

**706** WYR lose control of your legs every time you sneeze or every time you hear someone else sneeze?

**707** WYR wear wet jeans until they dry out or go ice skating with wet hair?

**708** WYR burn food or burn your fingers every time you cook?

**709** WYR build a Meccano (Erector) scale model of the Eiffel Tower or the Golden Gate Bridge?

**710** WYR have a scorpion's tail or a rattlesnake's tail?

**711** WYR be an orchestral conductor or the timpani (kettledrums) player in an orchestra?

**712** WYR jump rope or bounce on a trampoline?

**713** WYR feed the birds or water the plants?

**714** WYR walk through a giant cobweb or wade barefoot through frog spawn?

**715** WYR be pranked with worms as spaghetti or maggots as rice?

**716** WYR spend a rainy afternoon in a library or in a museum?

**717** WYR be able to visit Jurassic Park for real or be in *Night at the Museum* for real?

**718** WYR have the theme song from *Mission: Impossible* play every time you pee or the *Hawaii Five-O* theme?

**719** WYR spend a full day wearing snowshoes or wearing a beekeeper's hat?

**720** WYR sing-along so hard your voice cracks or laugh so hard your sides hurt?

**721** WYR avoid stepping on cracks on sidewalks or avoid opening an umbrella indoors?

**722** WYR be a pangolin or a penguin?

**723** WYR be a street sweeper or a crewmember on a navy minesweeper?

**724** WYR be a passenger stepping off the Mayflower into the New World or be Christopher Columbus setting sail across the Atlantic?

**725** WYR have fifteen children or fifteen dogs?

**726** WYR have an easy job working for someone else or work for yourself but work really hard?

**727** WYR be a chicken that barks like a dog or a hamster that clicks like a dolphin?

**728** WYR sketch and doodle or color?

**729** WYR be able to solve any math equation or able to fix any household gadget?

**730** WYR go out without brushing your hair or without brushing your teeth?

**731** WYR fight a Roman gladiator or a samurai warrior?

**732** WYR "build this city on rock and roll" or sausage rolls?

**733** WYR only shop on eBay or only shop on Amazon?

**734** WYR have a cassette-playing Sony Walkman instead of music downloads or a landline instead of a smartphone?

**735** WYR bring back Kenny Rogers in his prime or David Bowie?

**736** WYR comfort-eat with a whole carton of ice cream or a whole bucket of chicken wings?

**737** WYR have tea with Queen Elizabeth II or cocktails with Harry and Meghan?

**738** WYR be a pirate or a ninja for the weekend?

**739** WYR work with Homer Simpson or Stan Laurel?

**740** WYR drink water from the cat's water bowl or pee in the litter box?

**741** WYR only be able to watch the horror channel or the Christmas movie channel?

**742** WYR have an annoying song stuck in your head or the feeling you're about to sneeze for an hour?

**743** WYR do only indoor activities every weekend or only outdoor activities every weekend?

**744** WYR have a personal trainer or a personal chauffeur?

**745** WYR only eat sushi or only eat TV dinners?

**746** WYR have the strength of Superman or the speed of The Flash?

**747** WYR sleep on a public bathroom floor or on poison ivy?

**748** WYR learn an alien language or teach your language to an alien?

**749** WYR buy more than you need at the grocery store or forget the one thing you need?

**750** WYR lose your short-term memory or your long-term memory?

**751** WYR have rain on your wedding day or only have spoons when you need a knife?

**752** WYR be able to predict your own future or the future of the world?

**753** WYR live with a ghost in your house or be a ghost in someone else's house?

**754** WYR have a bath in dirty dishwater or wash dishes in dirty bathwater?

755 WYR be able to wipe your own memory or wipe someone else's memory, *Men in Black*-style?

756 WYR wear just one color or a mix of at least three colors every day?

757 WYR be ignored or have everything you say and do criticized?

758 WYR "Go West" with the Pet Shop Boys or stay at the "Hotel California" with the Eagles?

759 WYR clean up after every party you attend or never go to another party?

760 WYR only eat desserts for a year or not eat any desserts for two years?

761 WYR wear only neon pink or only neon yellow for a year?

762 WYR have a tennis lesson with Serena Williams or a golf lesson with Tiger Woods?

763 WYR be a punk rocker or a pink pony?

764 WYR live in a glass house with no blinds or a house with no windows?

765 WYR spectate at a *Punch and Judy* puppet show or dance at a barn dance?

766 WYR score the winning goal in the World Cup or be the coach of the winning team in the World Cup?

767 WYR have no power or no water in your home for a week?

768 WYR wake up in the gorilla enclosure in a zoo or in the wolf zone of a safari park?

769 WYR have Mr. Burns (*The Simpsons*) as your boss or Michael Scott (*The Office*)?

770 WYR be able to make vanish inconsiderate drivers or people who talk loudly on their phones in public places?

771 WYR never listen to music or only be able to listen to the same three songs?

772 WYR have a string of chart-topping hits or have a long musical career with no No. 1 hits?

773  WYR snack on chicken nuggets or donut holes?

774  WYR go back in time to meet Mohammad Ali in his prime or Jesse Owens in his prime?

775  WYR be a horse whisperer or a lion tamer?

776  WYR be a social media influencer or a community hero?

777  WYR look young when you're desperate to be older or look your age when you want to be younger?

778  WYR give or take bad advice?

779  WYR live forever but look your age or always look young but live an average length of life?

780  WYR have a fear of heights that keeps you on the first floor or a fear of the dark that means lights must stay on?

781  WYR become a cat or a dog?

782  WYR have an escalator or a travelator (moving walkway) in your home?

783  WYR live in a *Jetsons*-style home or a *Flintstones*-style home?

784  WYR eat at the Krusty Krab with SpongeBob or Arnold's diner with the Fonz?

785  WYR have the grace of a swan or the memory of an elephant?

786  WYR ride on the top deck of a double-decker bus or on the back of an elephant?

787  WYR have a guided tour of The White House or Buckingham Palace?

788  WYR only be able to communicate through charades or interpretive dance for a week?

789  WYR have your decisions made for you by other people or by tossing a coin?

790  WYR drink a gallon of ketchup or chew gum you found stuck under a table?

**791** WYR gain ten pounds in weight in a month or be banned from using social media for a month?

**792** WYR be a millionaire or have a superpower?

**793** WYR lose all the photos on your smartphone or lose your tickets for the big game?

**794** WYR lose the ability to high five or lose the ability to text?

**795** WYR speak like Siri or like Yoda?

**796** WYR have ears that can record what you hear or eyes that can record what you see?

**797** WYR be best friends with Kim Kardashian or Madonna?

**798** WYR have unlimited storage space in your home or on your computer?

**799** WYR be allergic to candy or to smartphones?

**800** WYR be a flightless bird or a non-venomous snake?

**801** WYR be a cowboy or a shepherd?

**802** WYR only be able to get into your car through a window or into your home through a window?

**803** WYR be a mountaineer or a mountain goat?

**804** WYR be a witch's familiar or a ship's mascot?

**805** WYR be a plant or a rock?

**806** WYR have ants in your pants or bugs in your bed?

**807** WYR be able to control the brightness of the sun or the temperature of food with a dial?

**808** WYR have a frozen shoulder or be given the cold shoulder?

**809** WYR only be able to play *Tetris* or *Pong*?

**810** WYR be able to pause time once a day or go back ten seconds once a day at will?

**811** WYR be a super sleuth or a super safecracker?

**812**   WYR have Iron Man's wealth and lifestyle or just his suit?

**813**   WYR eat what you want and never be overweight or never exercise and always be fit?

**814**   WYR have a personal robot or a flying carpet?

**815**   WYR go waterskiing or snowboarding?

**816**   WYR be a practicing doctor or a medical researcher?

**817**   WYR eat a raw potato or an undercooked boiled egg?

**818**   WYR fly a kite or fly in the face of danger?

**819**   WYR have a horse's head on your own body or a horse's body with your head?

**820**   WYR be stung by a bee or by ten mosquitos?

**821**   WYR have more time or more money?

**822**   WYR be able to change the length of your hair at will or snap your fingers to change outfits?

**823**   WYR meet a superhero or a cartoon character?

**824**   WYR be a spelling bee champion or a baton twirling champion?

**825**   WYR be an underwater creature with wings or a land animal with gills?

**826**   WYR spend a day playing paintball or laser tag?

**827**   WYR be one of Santa's elves or one of the shoemaker's elves?

**828**   WYR have a bugle fanfare as you enter a room or a drum roll before you speak?

**829**   WYR have breakfast at Tiffany's or tea at The Ritz?

**830**   WYR wallow in mud pie or chocolate pudding?

**831**   WYR kiss a dirty trash can or a frog?

**832**   WYR shovel snow for thirty minutes twice a day or rake leaves for one hour once a day?

**833** WYR be able to dodge anything no matter how fast it's moving or be able ask any three questions and have them answered accurately?

**834** WYR brush your teeth with soap or curdled milk?

**835** WYR travel by jetpack or flying car?

**836** WYR know the lyrics to every song or know the moves to every dance?

**837** WYR have one puppy or five kittens?

**838** WYR it was Christmas every day or your birthday every day?

**839** WYR be a maid for the untidiest person in the world or a chef for the fussiest eater in the world?

**840** WYR have a magic button that could stop other people from talking or stop other people from moving?

**841** WYR never feel pain or have your loved ones never feel pain?

**842** WYR have crooked white teeth or straight yellow-stained teeth?

**843** WYR fart loudly fifty times every day or pee your pants in public once a year?

**844** WYR eat a meal of gummy bears and sardines or liver and marshmallows?

**845** WYR be the captain of a debate team or the captain of a sports team?

**846** WYR have five cavities or five warts?

**847** WYR see something no one else can see or not see something everyone else can see?

**848** WYR wear a superhero cape or a pirate eyepatch?

**849** WYR travel at the speed of light or relax at the speed of a sloth?

**850** WYR drink out of a five-gallon bucket or a thimble?

**851** WYR be able to see smells or smell sounds?

**852** WYR have only picture books to read or subtitled movies to watch?

**853**   WYR be told you're adopted or that your siblings are adopted?

**854**   WYR have a house made of gingerbread or a tree that grows candy canes?

**855**   WYR be able to sketch things into existence or erase existing things with an eraser?

**856**   WYR run everywhere in a potato sack or always sleep in a sleeping bag?

**857**   WYR your breath smelled of garlic or you had food stains on your clothes?

**858**   WYR have the power to push things away using your eyes or pull things toward you using your eyes?

**859**   WYR accidentally spoil a movie for someone or have someone spoil a movie for you?

**860**   WYR be able to purr like a cat or trumpet like an elephant?

**861**   WYR have Pinocchio's nose or Dumbo's ears?

**862**   WYR be showered with Silly String or with confetti?

**863**   WYR walk on your hands or eat with your feet?

**864**   WYR own a prickly pet or a slimy pet?

**865**   WYR have antennae like a bug or smell with your tongue like a snake?

**866**   WYR be obliged to announce the imminent arrival of every burp or every fart before you do it?

**867**   WYR be trapped in a small space with five capuchin monkeys or twenty people?

**868**   WYR live on a pig's diet for a week or a shark's diet for a week?

**869**   WYR have a private paradise island or a private amusement park?

**870**   WYR eat a hamburger in a hotdog bun or a hotdog in a hamburger bun?

**871**   WYR live one long life of a thousand years or live ten different lives, each lasting a hundred years?

872 WYR have two spoonfuls of sugar or one spoonful of salt sprinkled on every meal you eat?

873 WYR be under the attack of a hundred snowballs or a hundred water balloons?

874 WYR stick your hand in a bucket of freezing cold water or a bucket of warm fish guts?

875 WYR be one of the Magnificent Seven or one of Ocean's Eleven?

876 WYR please others or please yourself?

877 WYR eat one cup of wet cat food in one meal or three cups of dry cat food across three meals?

878 WYR drink through your ears or eat through your belly button?

879 WYR have the power to shrink everything at will or make things double in size?

880 WYR have a pig's tail or a pug's tail?

881 WYR eat one cockroach or have one hundred cockroaches in your kitchen?

882 WYR be able to run like Roadrunner or eat like Scooby-Doo?

883 WYR drink like a cat or wash yourself like a cat?

884 WYR do the hokey pokey or join a conga line?

885 WYR trip and fall running toward someone or running away from someone?

886 WYR have soda spray out of your mouth or come down your nose when you laugh?

887 WYR be the first person to explore a planet or be the inventor of a drug that cures a deadly disease?

888 WYR be the last to know good news or the first to know bad news?

889 WYR look like a magazine front-cover model or be totally comfortable in your own skin?

890 WYR be the target for dodgeball practice or get six raw eggs cracked open on your head?

891 WYR run through sprinklers for fun or swing on a tree rope?

892 WYR use your non-dominant hand to write or to eat?

893 WYR never get tired or never have to go to the bathroom?

894 WYR go to clown school or agricultural college?

895 WYR grow new teeth like a shark or wear down your constantly growing teeth like a beaver?

896 WYR be subjected to hours of "She'll Be Coming Round the Mountain" or "The Diarrhea Song" on a long road trip?

897 WYR wear shoes on the wrong feet or shoes two sizes too big?

898 WYR catch the biggest fish on a fishing trip or the highest number of small fish?

899 WYR teleport to a different dimension or to a different country in this dimension?

900 WYR be the superhero or the superhero's indispensable sidekick?

901 WYR have an endless supply of Goldfish crackers or graham crackers?

902 WYR be bulletproof or have the power to catch bullets in your hands?

903 WYR be able to fly on a broomstick or have an invisibility cloak?

904 WYR have a dog's brain in a human body or a human brain in a dog's body?

905 WYR never be sad again or never be angry again?

906 WYR be a test pilot or a food tester?

907 WYR sleep with only a blanket or only a pillow?

908 WYR work in a sewage plant or a toxic chemicals plant?

909 WYR have a nose ring or a full sleeve tattoo?

910 WYR wear only flip flops in winter or only snow boots in summer?

911  WYR live in a house with a hall of mirrors or a concealed door in the bookcase?

912  WYR have to sit down all day in your job or stand up all day in your job?

913  WYR rise to the challenge of eating a pound of Skittles or a pound of Reese's Peanut Butter Cups?

914  WYR love animals but be allergic to them or not be allergic to animals but be frightened of them?

915  WYR have popsicles or ice cream if you could have only one?

916  WYR be a 1960s hippie or a 1920s flapper?

917  WYR never be rejected ever again or never fail ever again?

918  WYR sit next to someone who snores or someone who snaps their gum on a long-haul flight?

919  WYR have a time machine or a teleport machine?

920  WYR be the director of a Hollywood blockbuster or have twenty million subscribers to your YouTube channel?

921  WYR be totally alone for a year or never be alone for a year?

922  WYR fall off a real bucking bronco or fall off a mechanical bull?

923  WYR only be able to listen to rap music or songs from Broadway musicals?

924  WYR have a starring role in a TV drama or a supporting role in a Hollywood movie?

925  WYR be a game show host or a standup comedian?

926  WYR win an Academy Award or an Olympic medal?

927  WYR figure things out for yourself or ask for help?

928  WYR freefall into the Grand Canyon with a parachute or run across a river on the backs of alligators?

929  WYR have a booger in your nose that moves in and out when you breathe or sneeze a booger onto someone?

**930** WYR have cookies or cake if you could only have one?

**931** WYR be a character in *The Wizard of Oz* or *The Sound of Music*?

**932** WYR be an actor doing your own stunts or a stuntman doing stunts for actors?

**933** WYR suffer from unpredictable fits of giggles or spontaneous moments of talking like a pirate?

**934** WYR lick the bottom of your shoe or wear someone else's sweaty socks?

**935** WYR have stitches or have a dislocated shoulder popped back in without anesthetic?

**936** WYR cry tears of lemonade or sneeze cheese?

**937** WYR be true to yourself or fake it till you make it?

**938** WYR lie to your family or lie to your friends?

**939** WYR argue until the cows come home or walk away from an argument?

**940** WYR get caught in a swarm of crickets or an army of ants?

**941** WYR own a restaurant chain or a hotel chain?

**942** WYR have a broken foot or a broken hand?

**943** WYR spill a pot of silver glitter on a black carpet or a pot of paprika on a white carpet?

**944** WYR be a ski instructor or a surf instructor?

**945** WYR bring back Abraham Lincoln or JFK?

**946** WYR be able to navigate using the stars or tell the time using the sun?

**947** WYR go back to age five with everything you know now or know now everything your future self will learn?

**948** WYR be a parkour master or a master chef?

**949** WYR have a hairdryer or a vacuum cleaner that lacks power?

**950** WYR a movie was made of your life since the age of twenty-one or before the age of twenty-one?

**951** WYR have constant dull pain or a constant itch?

**952** WYR never be able to ask another question or never be able to answer another question?

**953** WYR live in Narnia or the Pokémon universe?

**954** WYR hold the world record for holding your breath or for holding the longest singing note?

**955** WYR discover where the missing socks go or find $50 down the back of the sofa?

**956** WYR go to work in a tutu or in traditional German lederhosen?

**957** WYR read everything out loud or speak your thoughts out loud?

**958** WYR do a TED talk or sing a song on stage at a concert with your favorite singer?

**959** WYR inherit $20 million or earn $150 million through your hard work?

**960** WYR spend a night in a teepee or an igloo?

**961** WYR blow up one hundred party balloons without a pump or wash ten cars by hand?

**962** WYR lose three friends or gain an enemy?

**963** WYR have duck feet or go for a swim before every meal?

**964** WYR end crime or end poverty?

**965** WYR be eliminated from *Survivor* or *The X Factor*?

**966** WYR wake up and be unable to see your reflection in a mirror or not recognize the person you see in the mirror?

**967** WYR be a barnacle on a whale or a starfish on a rock?

**968** WYR get free iTunes for life or get free tickets to see your favorite band in concert?

**969** WYR have it all or know it all?

970 WYR get bad sunburn or fall into stinging nettles wearing only a swimsuit?

971 WYR sleep in a hammock or sleep on a mattress on the floor?

972 WYR have a pillow fight or a midnight feast?

973 WYR visit Universal Studios or Epcot Center?

974 WYR run with bulls in Spain or walk on the Great Wall of China?

975 WYR share a room with the world's loudest snorer or give up chocolate?

976 WYR lose your wallet or lose all the photos on your phone?

977 WYR spend the night alone in a wax museum or a morgue?

978 WYR have a face like a cat or a monkey's tail for a week?

979 WYR never move from the house you grew up in or move into a different house every two years?

980 WYR be the bull rider at the rodeo or the clown that distracts the bull when the rider falls?

981 WYR meet an Ent (*The Lord of the Rings*) or the BFG?

982 WYR wear a swim cap or a nose plug to work for a week?

983 WYR own a dragon or be a dragon?

984 WYR get your hand stuck in a jar or a pot stuck on your head?

985 WYR hold a grudge or let bygones be bygones?

986 WYR talk like Daffy Duck or Bugs Bunny?

987 WYR live a dog's life or have a cat's nine lives?

988 WYR drink hot sauce or eat a stick of butter?

989 WYR never laugh again or sound like Woody Woodpecker every time you laughed?

990 WYR sit through a movie you're not enjoying or pay for a meal you don't enjoy?

**991** WYR be a real-world magician or a wizard in a fantasy world?

**992** WYR wake up as a character in your favorite anime or wake up to a pot of gold on your pillow?

**993** WYR have a missing finger or an extra toe?

**994** WYR have 10,000 spiders invade your bedroom or one elephant?

**995** WYR be Jack Sparrow or Luke Skywalker for a day?

**996** WYR go to prison for your best friend's crime or have your best friend go to prison for your crime?

**997** WYR everyone had to backflip into meeting rooms or cartwheel out of meeting rooms?

**998** WYR have a big bedroom or a big bed?

**999** WYR blow your own horn or hide your light under a bushel?

**1000** WYR eat a ladybug or be a litterbug?

**1001** WYR be the tree or the treehouse?

**1002** WYR have a suitcase full of dollars or a blood-stained knife in your car when pulled over by a police officer?

**1003** WYR misread everything you read or mispronounce everything you say?

**1004** WYR be able to solve every sudoku puzzle or complete every crossword?

**1005** WYR be Highlander (Connor MacLeod) or Wolverine?

**1006** WYR be a traditional Chinese lion dancer or dance with your dog?

**1007** WYR get eggs fresh from your own chickens or milk fresh from your own cow?

**1008** WYR have Uncle Buck or Mrs. Doubtfire as your babysitter?

**1009** WYR never be credited or take the credit for someone else's efforts?

**1010** WYR have lived in the times of *Gone with the Wind* or the times of *Casablanca*?

**1011**  WYR read *War and Peace* in its entirety or run two marathons?

**1012**  WYR do your laundry by hand for a week or cut an acre of grass with a manual push mower?

**1013**  WYR have green fingers or blue blood?

**1014**  WYR work eight hours a day in a job you love or four hours a day in a job you hate?

**1015**  WYR everyone looked the same or everyone had the same name?

**1016**  WYR have two kittens in mittens or one puss in boots?

**1017**  WYR walk a mile in someone else's shoes or a mile in stilettos?

**1018**  WYR roast chestnuts on an open fire or ride a chestnut horse?

**1019**  WYR build a bridge or burn a bridge?

**1020**  WYR punish thieves by putting them in ye olde stocks or punish irresponsible drivers by putting them on the ducking stool?

**1021**  WYR be reincarnated as a bee or a tree?

**1022**  WYR have a sparrow's nest in your hair or a wasps' nest in your bedroom?

**1023**  WYR speak in rhyme or speak in riddles?

**1024**  WYR have first pick or have the last laugh?

**1025**  WYR speak an ancient (dead) language or construct a new language?

**1026**  WYR be held in high regard by your parents or by your friends?

**1027**  WYR be happy and you know it or be beautiful and not know it?

**1028**  WYR have a wolf at the door or not be able to get your foot in the door?

**1029**  WYR make an entrance or pussyfoot around?

**1030**  WYR have a flying carpet or a car that can drive underwater?

**1031**  WYR pit yourself against Canadian wildlife or Australian wildlife in a survival situation?

**1032**  WYR have a bad taste in your mouth or smell a bit funky?

**1033**  WYR have Old MacDonald's Farm or Winnie the Pooh's Hundred Acre Wood?

**1034**  WYR be snug as a bug in a rug or cool as a cucumber?

**1035**  WYR watch the *Emoji* movie twice back-to-back or listen to muzak (elevator music) for a whole day?

**1036**  WYR have been a famous actor in the 1980s or a famous singer in the 1990s?

**1037**  WYR be Clark Kent without his Superman powers or Peter Parker without his Spiderman powers?

**1038**  WYR be anonymous or eponymous and give your name to something?

**1039**  WYR eat only Italian food for the rest of your life or only Mexican food?

**1040**  WYR be a prisoner in Azkaban or Alcatraz?

**1041**  WYR get your way or go with the flow?

**1042**  WYR be an average person in the present or a king of a large country 2500 years ago?

**1043**  WYR risk eating tomato-based pasta sauce or drinking red berry juice when wearing an all-white outfit?

**1044**  WYR have the power to control your dreams or control the dreams of others?

**1045**  WYR drink milk straight from a cow or eat raw steak?

**1046**  WYR be a mad scientist or a computer-hacking genius?

**1047**  WYR drive a tank or pilot a fighter jet?

**1048**  WYR ride into battle on a warhorse or in a chariot?

**1049**  WYR be able to ice skate on sidewalks or have waterslides on sidewalks?

**1050**  WYR have free popcorn at the movies for life or free tickets to any movie for a year?

1051 WYR have a cat with nine tails or a llama with two heads?

1052 WYR have a pet that can talk to you (only you) or a pet that never dies?

1053 WYR celebrate Thanksgiving twice a year or the 4th of July twice a year?

1054 WYR have an invisibility cloak or a spaceship with a cloaking device?

1055 WYR be a space pirate or an eighteenth-century smuggler?

1056 WYR be a police officer with a flying motorcycle or a police officer with a talking dog?

1057 WYR be feared by all or loved by all?

1058 WYR never be able to eat nachos again or never be able to eat Cheetos again?

1059 WYR only be able to eat when it's dark outside or only be able to sleep when it's light outside?

1060 WYR have a chicken that lays chocolate eggs or a cow that gives strawberry milk?

1061 WYR have been in charge of building Stonehenge or the Egyptian pyramids?

1062 WYR have gravy on cookies or custard on potato chips?

1063 WYR live in a world with no crime or no lies?

1064 WYR live in a cupboard under the stairs like Harry Potter or in a pineapple under the sea like SpongeBob SquarePants?

1065 WYR your closet door led to Monstropolis (*Monsters, Inc.*) or Narnia?

1066 WYR be forgetful or clumsy?

1067 WYR play baseball with a basketball or football with a tennis ball?

1068 WYR be a professional belly dancer or a professional limbo dancer?

1069 WYR wake up to a *Planet of the Apes* world or an *Independence Day* world?

**1070** WYR run across America like Forrest Gump or run in the U.S. presidential election?

**1071** WYR wear weighted deep-sea diving boots all day or operate keyboards with your feet?

**1072** WYR live in a spacious one-level loft apartment or a three-story mansion?

**1073** WYR be a theme park ride designer or a wedding planner?

**1074** WYR be a wild hare or have great hair?

**1075** WYR bring back an extinct species or prevent another species from becoming extinct?

**1076** WYR have a guide dog or a guide toucan?

**1077** WYR be unable to talk once a day for an hour or be unable to talk for a year?

**1078** WYR eat a hundred apples or drink a hundred pints of milk?

**1079** WYR everything smelled like freshly mown grass or cotton candy?

**1080** WYR a house-elf moved into your bedroom or a friendly under-the-bed monster?

**1081** WYR become a Transformer or have rocket boots for a day?

**1082** WYR eat a bag of dog treats or drink a glass of hot dog water?

**1083** WYR a story you're writing became reality or a story you're reading became reality?

**1084** WYR every argument in the world was settled with rock paper scissors or the weather was decided with a coin toss?

**1085** WYR have a magic self-refilling fridge or be able to memorize everything you see and hear?

**1086** WYR exercise by walking on a treadmill or juggling oranges for thirty minutes every day?

**1087** WYR have Knight Rider's Kitt or Herbie the Love Bug?

**1088** WYR be a paramedic or a private eye?

**1089** WYR count out loud to a billion once or climb up the 1,576 stairs of the Empire State Building twice in one day?

**1090** WYR have a foam party or a BBQ on the beach?

**1091** WYR have fangs or a crooked smile?

**1092** WYR clean a public restroom without gloves or walk through a cow field without socks and shoes?

**1093** WYR be a full-time clown or a full-time steeplejack?

**1094** WYR be face to face with a shark in a submerged shark cage or eat pufferfish (fugu)?

**1095** WYR be a Muppet in *The Muppet Movie* or a Fraggle on *Fraggle Rock*?

**1096** WYR run a post office or an office supply store?

**1097** WYR be able to see five minutes into the future or five years into the future?

**1098** WYR have unshakeable will power or have a credit card with no limit?

**1099** WYR become a ghost or a zombie when you die?

**1100** WYR be the spy in a spy novel or the mole in an organization?

**1101** WYR be obsessive and meticulous or haphazard and nonchalant?

**1102** WYR have Mickey Mouse's *Fantasia* broomstick or Cinderella's helpful bluebirds?

**1103** WYR wear the Cat in the Hat's hat or Jack Sparrow's hat?

**1104** WYR be feared or be fearless?

**1105** WYR sweep things under the rug or risk opening a can of worms?

**1106** WYR never have to barf again or never have constipation ever again?

**1107** WYR spend the day in a beautiful location on a rainy day or a dull location on a sunny day?

**1108** WYR be a hamster on a wheel or a ferret in a tunnel?

**1109**  WYR crack open a rotten egg or spill rotten milk?

**1110**  WYR be a practical person or a dreamer?

**1111**  WYR wake up as a giant cockroach or a giant snail?

**1112**  WYR win a three-minute shopping cart dash in a candy store or win a lifetime pass for your local gym?

**1113**  WYR spend a day washing glass windows or wearing glass shoes?

**1114**  WYR have a dog named Cat or a cat that needs to be walked on a lead like a dog?

**1115**  WYR have the eyes of a painting follow you around a room or be secretly filmed by a hidden camera?

**1116**  WYR have a hat that turned into a helicopter or shoes that turned into a jet ski?

**1117**  WYR ride a desert train or a ghost train?

**1118**  WYR drink only cranberry juice or only milk?

**1119**  WYR meet Will Smith as the Fresh Prince of Bel-Air or Agent J (*Men in Black*)?

**1120**  WYR sticks and stones could never break your bones or names could never hurt you?

**1121**  WYR your hair grew to ankle-length every two days or changed color every day?

**1122**  WYR never have to sleep again or be able to take a nap whenever you want?

**1123**  WYR love or be loved?

**1124**  WYR have the best headphones in the world or be able to play music at any volume anywhere and anytime?

**1125**  WYR hug or fist bump?

**1126**  WYR all food looked the same or tasted the same?

**1127**  WYR have to wear hi-vis clothing or a hairnet at your job?

**1128**  WYR be liked or be respected?

**1129** WYR be the world's best bread maker or the world's best cake baker?

**1130** WYR never get another mosquito bite or never get another paper cut?

**1131** WYR be compelled to shout "Boogers!" or "Cowabunga!" every time you enter a building?

**1132** WYR have a nose the size of your fist or hands the size of your nose?

**1133** WYR spread mayo or strawberry jam on everything you eat?

**1134** WYR host a late-night TV talk show or a radio breakfast show?

**1135** WYR paint the town red or be tickled pink?

**1136** WYR be a free spirit or know your sole purpose in life?

**1137** WYR swim with Willy the orca or hang out with Beethoven the dog?

**1138** WYR be able to control when and how you laugh or when and how you cry?

**1139** WYR be poor but help people or become rich by hurting people?

**1140** WYR do whatever it takes or have the moral high ground?

**1141** WYR hug a tall cactus (saguaro) or roll in a nettle patch?

**1142** WYR visit the Little House on the Prairie or the Little Shop of Horrors?

**1143** WYR play Snap with cards or play games on Snapchat?

**1144** WYR sit in the back seat on a bus or the front seat on a rollercoaster?

**1145** WYR be tongue-tied or be a blabbermouth?

**1146** WYR have greater intelligence or greater wisdom?

**1147** WYR experience being your ninety-year-old self or return to being your nine-year-old self for a day?

**1148** WYR surprise someone by baking them a cake or have someone surprise you by jumping out of a cake?

**1149** WYR everyone had to wear a monochrome uniform or everyone had to wear 1960s fashion clothing?

**1150** WYR be Woody or Buzz Lightyear in *Toy Story*?

**1151** WYR be the queen bee or king of the hill?

**1152** WYR have a song written about you or have your life story written?

**1153** WYR eat twenty pounds of cheese in one sitting or drink a gallon of ketchup in a day?

**1154** WYR be a dentist or have to visit the dentist once a month?

**1155** WYR kiss a jellyfish or shake hands with your worst enemy?

**1156** WYR be able to change the world or just change the way your life panned out in the last year?

**1157** WYR have bulging eyes or bow legs?

**1158** WYR know the true meaning of love or the meaning of life?

**1159** WYR live in a world controlled by robots or a world with no formal education?

**1160** WYR do things right or do the right thing?

**1161** WYR live in a world without guns or a world without social media?

**1162** WYR there was only one global language or everyone had to be multilingual?

**1163** WYR be physically stronger or have better concentration abilities?

**1164** WYR have total control or leave things to chance?

**1165** WYR have more time or more power?

**1166** WYR live under a sky with no stars at night or live under a sky with no clouds during the day?

**1167** WYR campaign for free trade or fair trade?

**1168** WYR have high self-esteem or always have a shoulder to cry on?

1169 WYR be a dog with its head out of a moving car window or a kitten chasing a ball of wool?

1170 WYR never be embarrassed again or never cry again?

1171 WYR already have everything you want or be able to afford anything you want?

1172 WYR never cheat or cheat only if you knew you couldn't be found out?

1173 WYR fall madly in love with everyone you meet or feel deeply suspicious of everyone you meet?

1174 WYR have great mental health but poor physical health or great physical health but poor mental health?

1175 WYR be responsible for sending an innocent person to prison or for letting a guilty person go free?

1176 WYR wake up speaking with a Russian accent or a French accent?

1177 WYR not be able to get a haircut for six months or not be able to watch TV for six months?

1178 WYR be a happy person for only fifty percent of your life or be a totally happy dog?

1179 WYR legalize euthanasia or make organ donation mandatory?

1180 WYR never have to clean a bathroom again or never have to do dishes again?

1181 WYR be the mouse that ran up the clock or the itsy-bitsy spider?

1182 WYR trust your intuition or trust the opinions of friends and family?

1183 WYR be confident as a leader or happy as a follower?

1184 WYR be able to save money or be able to give money away?

1185 WYR learn through reading or experimenting?

1186 WYR have superficial knowledge of most things or a deep knowledge of a few things?

**1187** WYR eat rice with every meal and never be able to eat bread or eat bread with every meal and never be able to eat rice?

**1188** WYR wake up tomorrow with a Marvel-style superpower or with Gandalf-style magical abilities?

**1189** WYR settle for what you already know or keep on asking more questions?

**1190** WYR live ten more years with excellent health or live thirty more years with declining health?

**1191** WYR have a plan or fly by the seat of your pants?

**1192** WYR choose a partner through looks or brains?

**1193** WYR be left alone when you're feeling down or have someone cheer you up?

**1194** WYR never be brokenhearted or never break someone's heart?

**1195** WYR walk in the moonlight or run in the sun?

**1196** WYR cry crocodile tears or cry wolf?

**1197** WYR be where you are now or be anywhere other than where you are now?

**1198** WYR be an honest simpleton or a dishonest genius?

**1199** WYR super sensitive taste or super sensitive hearing?

**1200** WYR learn the hard way or never make a mistake?

**1201** WYR be a teacher of one thing or a student of many things?

**1202** WYR do what you love or love what you're doing?

**1203** WYR do your own thing or be in with the in-crowd?

**1204** WYR sell all of your possessions or sell one of your organs?

**1205** WYR relive yesterday just as it was or relive it to change it?

**1206** WYR have greater responsibility or get rid of some of your responsibilities?

**1207** WYR your shirts were two sizes too big or one size too small?

**1208** WYR go it alone or have a sidekick?

**1209** WYR watch less TV or spend less time online?

**1210** WYR know when it's time to give in and let go or never quit?

**1211** WYR believe nothing is impossible or believe there's no place like home?

**1212** WYR believe only what you see or see whatever you put your mind to?

**1213** WYR forget a memorable day or forfeit a valuable prize?

**1214** WYR lose your mojo or lose your marbles?

**1215** WYR burn rubber or have money to burn?

**1216** WYR be more like your mom or more like your dad?

**1217** WYR be able to remember every dream or forget every nightmare?

**1218** WYR never experience loneliness or never have your trust broken?

**1219** WYR go for the easy option or go for the luxury choice?

**1220** WYR visit the Inventing Room in Willy Wonka's Chocolate Factory or the BFG's dream collection in his cave?

**1221** WYR have hands that kept growing or feet that kept growing?

**1222** WYR audition for *America's Got Talent* or *The Voice*?

**1223** WYR swap lives with your favorite celebrity or a character from a book you've read?

**1224** WYR buy things on impulse or write a shopping list and stick to it?

**1225** WYR keep the name you have or permanently change your name?

**1226** WYR only be able to watch reality TV shows on your TV or take part in one?

**1227** WYR keep your own secret or keep a friend's secret for life?

**1228** WYR be a male midwife or a female construction worker?

**1229** WYR have an old banger that gets you around or save up until you can get a better car?

**1230** WYR go back on your word or eat your words?

**1231** WYR write someone a love letter or confess how you feel face to face?

**1232** WYR believe in fate or believe that nothing happens unless you make it happen?

**1233** WYR play hopscotch or make a cootie catcher?

**1234** WYR never be able to smell your favorite scent again or never smell the aroma of your favorite food again?

**1235** WYR never be hated or never be wrong?

**1236** WYR have been born during World War I or during World War II?

**1237** WYR have the sports car of your dreams or go on a road trip with your three best friends?

**1238** WYR invite three celebrity guests or three historical figures to dinner?

**1239** WYR only be able to listen to the music you loved ten years ago or watch the TV shows you loved ten years ago?

**1240** WYR never be annoyed by anyone ever again or never lose your patience ever again?

**1241** WYR be in a three-month lockdown situation with the smartest person you know or the funniest person you know?

**1242** WYR learn how to home-cook your favorite restaurant meal or only have it once a year at a restaurant?

**1243** WYR be rewarded for an act of heroism or for winning an international competition?

**1244** WYR relive a year of your life or have no memories of a year in your life?

**1245** WYR spend a day on a nude beach or have an embarrassing photo of you shared on social media?

**1246** WYR eat the same foods at every meal for a month or eat at exactly the same mealtimes for a month?

**1247** WYR live a movie moment or meet your favorite movie star?

**1248** WYR be unpopular or be popular for doing something you're not proud of?

**1249** WYR stick with tradition or never be governed by any tradition?

**1250** WYR use your last wish to achieve a personal dream or to free the genie from the bottle?

**1251** WYR have an audio recording of you singing in the shower or a video of you baking a cake shared on social media?

**1252** WYR play a board game or a video game?

**1253** WYR treat yourself by eating your favorite dessert or by buying a new item of clothing?

**1254** WYR have an evening out at a comedy club or in a nightclub?

**1255** WYR scuba dive or stage dive?

**1256** WYR trip and fall as you step up to give a presentation or forget what you're saying halfway through a presentation?

**1257** WYR become a millionaire or get to live in the fictional world of your favorite movie?

**1258** WYR quantum leap into an unknown future or beam down (*Star Trek*-style) onto an unknown planet?

**1259** WYR eat stale potato chips or stale breakfast cereal?

**1260** WYR have Thor's hammer or the Helmet of Hades (Cap of Invisibility)?

**1261** WYR die in twenty years with no regrets or die in fifty with many regrets?

**1262** WYR meet Taylor Swift or Bruce Springsteen?

**1263** WYR hang out with Snoopy or Garfield?

**1264** WYR relive your most embarrassing moment in life so far or give up the internet for six months?

**1265** WYR hear voices in your head or see dead people?

**1266** WYR eat cheese with live maggots or eat live sea urchin?

**1267** WYR explore an underwater cave or an underground tunnel?

**1268** WYR have no sense of humor or no sense of danger?

**1269** WYR be agoraphobic or a germaphobe?

**1270** WYR be a long-distance swimmer or a cross-country skier?

**1271** WYR have the most beautiful eyes or the most amazing smile?

**1272** WYR have a horrible job, but be able to retire comfortably in ten years or have your dream job, but work until you die?

**1273** WYR have a job that starts at 4 am or one that starts at 4 pm?

**1274** WYR be a garbage collector or a celebrity whom people love to hate?

**1275** WYR know what the future holds for you or know what the future holds for your family members?

**1276** WYR live a nomadic lifestyle or settle in one place?

**1277** WYR have political power but be poor or be rich but have no political power?

**1278** WYR spend a day as the person you are now but in the 1950s or in the 1970s?

**1279** WYR party hard every night or never party again?

**1280** WYR have a secret lair or a private jet?

**1281** WYR have lunch with Warren Buffet or Madonna?

**1282** WYR be covered in hair or be completely bald?

**1283** WYR take early retirement or keep working on something until your dying day?

**1284** WYR come back in another life as an energetic dog or a lazy cat?

**1285** WYR never feel guilty again or never feel awkward again?

**1286** WYR live in an area with slow internet or an unreliable cellphone signal?

**1287** WYR answer your phone or let messages go to voicemail?

**1288** WYR have bright lighting or soft lighting in your home if you could have only one?

**1289** WYR be known by a catchphrase or a signature move?

**1290** WYR never eat pizza again or never eat burgers again?

**1291** WYR have a bad hair day or a gassy day?

**1292** WYR have the power to wipe an annoying celebrity you can't stand from existence or a band?

**1293** WYR be able to punch someone in the face and get away with it or pretend to be someone else and get away with it?

**1294** WYR wish on a star or at a wishing well?

**1295** WYR explore a new city on foot with a guide or take a bus tour around a city?

**1296** WYR go on a hunting trip or go to a yoga retreat?

**1297** WYR keep money you found in a taxi or give it to the taxi driver?

**1298** WYR spend a gift of $5,000 on travel or on clothes and entertainment?

**1299** WYR watch a horror movie on your own or watch a show you want to concentrate on with noisy friends?

**1300** WYR it was the day after tomorrow or the day before yesterday?

**1301** WYR be the person you are today or become a different version of you?

**1302** WYR sleep an hour less than you need or go to bed an hour too early?

**1303** WYR meet your doppelganger or meet the doppelganger of someone you know?

**1304** WYR be a sleepwalker or a sleep talker?

**1305** WYR never kill a spider or never step on a crack?

**1306** WYR do a dumpster dive or go metal detecting?

**1307** WYR swallow gum or swallow a fly?

**1308** WYR go for a swim immediately after a heavy meal or run with scissors in your hand?

**1309** WYR be guilty of a traffic violation or of offending the fashion police on social media?

**1310** WYR have your family turn into clowns or chimpanzees?

**1311** WYR watch *Keeping Up with the Kardashians* or listen to Justin Bieber songs?

**1312** WYR play Whac-A-Mole or ring-a-bottle at a carnival?

**1313** WYR never make fun of someone ever again or never have others poke fun at you?

**1314** WYR pursue a pie-in-the-sky idea or chase a red herring?

**1315** WYR be able to do a one-handed handstand or a one-armed push-up?

**1316** WYR bite your tongue or stub your toe?

**1317** WYR fall asleep in the cinema or fall asleep on public transport?

**1318** WYR be born rich in a poor country or be born into a royal family and a life of duty?

**1319** WYR have your face on a $100 bill or be the face of an iconic brand?

**1320** WYR go to sleep knowing there's a mosquito in the room or suspecting there may be a rat in the walls?

**1321** WYR be the first line of defense or the last line?

**1322** WYR be the voice of a lead character in an animated movie or have a bit part in a popular live-action movie?

**1323** WYR have an alien friend or an invisible friend?

**1324** WYR live in a windmill or a lighthouse?

1325  WYR have Rolanda Hooch or Pomona Sprout as your teacher?

1326  WYR walk on your toes in ballet shoes or wear fishermen's chest waders?

1327  WYR go on a date with Hannibal Lecter or Norman Bates?

1328  WYR stop to smell the flowers or be a rolling stone that gathers no moss?

1329  WYR have lunch with Neil Armstrong or Andy Warhol?

1330  WYR have your crime novel murderer dispose of the body in a shallow grave or by chopping it into pieces?

1331  WYR start every sentence with "As I was saying . . ." or end every sentence with ". . . don't you know"?

1332  WYR have a Yule log cake at Easter or a chocolate egg at Christmas?

1333  WYR have "Daydream Believer" by the Monkees or "Beautiful" by Christina Aguilera on the soundtrack of your life?

1334  WYR wear clashing colors or a jester's hat?

1335  WYR memorize and know the flags of every country in the world or memorize the lyrics to every Pink Floyd song?

1336  WYR randomly scream at the top of your voice or randomly leap in the air once a day?

1337  WYR have the chance to ask George Washington one question or Elvis Presley one question?

1338  WYR wear shoes that don't match your outfit or wear casual shoes with a formal outfit?

1339  WYR hang out with Hong Kong Phooey or the Foo Fighters?

1340  WYR bring back Kurt Cobain on Heath Ledger?

1341  WYR have your worst enemy read your diary or have all the pictures on your phone posted online?

1342  WYR have the feeling you're being followed or know you're being gossiped about?

**1343** WYR never see your best friend again or never see your pet again?

**1344** WYR empty the water from a swimming pool using a cup or count the grains of sand in a sandcastle?

**1345** WYR give up junk food forever or drink one cup of pee?

**1346** WYR have to flee a forest fire or a plague of locusts?

**1347** WYR have bright orange knees or bright blue elbows?

**1348** WYR eat a gallon of rocky road ice cream or an entire birthday cake in one sitting?

**1349** WYR live in a cottage by a lake or in a houseboat on a lake?

**1350** WYR have friends who are more attractive than you or who are smarter than you?

**1351** WYR be the person who prevented a war or the person who ended a war?

**1352** WYR have a weird laugh or a weird sense of humor?

**1353** WYR have tentacles instead of arms or instead of legs?

**1354** WYR have a round face or a square head?

**1355** WYR have a hoverboard or inline skates?

**1356** WYR have a thousand people follow you on Instagram or $1,000?

**1357** WYR have a gap between your front teeth or pointed ears?

**1358** WYR be chased by an angry bee or an agitated seagull?

**1359** WYR be sixteen forever or thirty-five forever?

**1360** WYR have a house party or party in the park?

**1361** WYR volunteer in an animal shelter or at a children's home?

**1362** WYR never be able to watch football again or never be able to shoot hoops again?

**1363** WYR drink a glass of vinegar or eat a block of butter?

**1364** WYR never read a book again or never go bowling again?

**1365** WYR switch bodies with the person on your right or switch heads with the person on your left?

**1366** WYR be slapped across the face with a wet fish or licked on the face by a slobbery dog?

**1367** WYR have no internet after 5 pm every day or only be able to send three text messages in a day?

**1368** WYR only be able to receive telephone calls or only make calls and not receive them?

**1369** WYR relax by sitting in a jacuzzi or by getting a massage?

**1370** WYR be overweight or constantly under pressure?

**1371** WYR be a champion waffle maker or a champion waffler?

**1372** WYR have sand in your shoes or cookie crumbs in your bed?

**1373** WYR only be able to wear purple for a month or only be able to eat white-colored foods for a week?

**1374** WYR be a stock market trader or a flea market trader?

**1375** WYR donate $5 to charity or take a chance on winning more by buying scratch-off cards?

**1376** WYR wear a hat or a belt as your statement accessory?

**1377** WYR eat birds to survive or eat bird seed to survive?

**1378** WYR have been on board Apollo 13 or US Airways Flight 1549 (Miracle on the Hudson)?

**1379** WYR be a cork bobbing on the ocean or a feather floating in the breeze?

**1380** WYR pretend you're sick to get out of going somewhere or pretend to get a call to get out of a conversation?

**1381** WYR drink tea from a cup and saucer or from a mug?

**1382** WYR be out of your depth or out of time?

**1383** WYR see a chimpanzee riding on a Segway or a monkey riding backwards on a pig?

**1384** WYR have Indiana Jones's whip or Lara Croft's pistols?

**1385** WYR it was raining tacos or hailing taquitos?

**1386** WYR never get another haircut or never eat breakfast again?

**1387** WYR your bedroom had the aroma of aged cheese or wet dog?

**1388** WYR live in luxury in New York or in luxury in Los Angeles?

**1389** WYR be lost in a cornfield or lost in a shopping mall?

**1390** WYR take on an all-you-can-eat challenge or a hot-and-spicy food challenge?

**1391** WYR live in a world with no evil people or a world with no disease?

**1392** WYR be targeted by Pennywise or Chucky?

**1393** WYR live without YouTube or without Netflix?

**1394** WYR keep your finger on the pulse or let the world pass you by?

**1395** WYR climb the corporate ladder or climb trees?

**1396** WYR only have a shower at home or only have a bathtub at home?

**1397** WYR be abducted by aliens or kidnapped by vampires?

**1398** WYR learn how to dance the fandango or learn how to cook a soufflé?

**1399** WYR have chocolate-flavored toothpaste or have chocolate sauce on fries?

**1400** WYR play solitaire or blackjack?

**1401** WYR have a lifetime supply of shampoo or breakfast cereal?

**1402** WYR add a new word to the dictionary or discover a new planet?

**1403** WYR read eBooks or listen to podcasts?

**1404** WYR sleep with the AC on or with the windows open?

**1405** WYR play Guess Who or Battleship?

**1406** WYR teach a parrot to talk or a dog to dance?

1407   WYR eat breakfast or lunch if you could eat only once a day?

1408   WYR have a career mentor or a life coach?

1409   WYR go to a family reunion or a school reunion?

1410   WYR have family you consider friends or friends you consider family?

1411   WYR direct a movie or star in a movie?

1412   WYR get it right the first time every time or be given a second chance every time?

1413   WYR read a newspaper or watch the news on TV?

1414   WYR take over the family business or start your own business?

1415   WYR be a cancer survivor or the lone survivor of a train wreck?

1416   WYR walk around a puddle or splash through a puddle?

1417   WYR drink iced coffee in the winter or hot chocolate in the summer?

1418   WYR win your height in books or your weight in gummy bears?

1419   WYR share a box of chicken nuggets with Usain Bolt or a pizza with Michael Phelps?

1420   WYR put peanut butter on jelly or jelly on peanut butter?

1421   WYR change something about yourself or change something about the world?

1422   WYR be able to have a conversation with your favorite stuffed animal or with people in paintings?

1423   WYR give up watching TV and movies for one year or give up playing video games for one year?

1424   WYR have the power to ban a particular fashion trend or ban TV shows?

1425   WYR have to wear wet clothes every day for a week or have dry lips for a month?

**1426** WYR look at the stars in the night sky or listen to waves lapping on the shore?

**1427** WYR be a master impersonator or a master ventriloquist?

**1428** WYR be Pikachu or Rin-Tin-Tin?

**1429** WYR be free as a bird or happy as a lark?

**1430** WYR let your friends pick a tattoo for you or pick your outfits for you every day for a year?

**1431** WYR pretend to be into something you're not to impress someone or pretend not to like something you do?

**1432** WYR be an interior designer in The White House or in Buckingham Palace?

**1433** WYR be "at home with the Osbournes" or "outdoors with the Morgans"?

**1434** WYR get paid to endorse a brand you don't like or be a movie critic?

**1435** WYR be Secret Squirrel or Danger Mouse?

**1436** WYR have a tank or a T-Rex on your side as you go into battle?

**1437** WYR be stalked by Freddy Krueger or Jason Voorhees?

**1438** WYR help a loved one cover up a crime or give up your beloved pet if a loved one became allergic?

**1439** WYR be abducted by aliens or get stuck to an airplane toilet seat mid-flight?

**1440** WYR never look stupid or never take yourself too seriously?

**1441** WYR spend a night in the Overlook Hotel (*The Shining*) or Bates Motel (*Psycho*)?

**1442** WYR sleepwalk onto a busy freeway or onto the roof of a tall building?

**1443** WYR be a survivor in a *Zombieland* world or *A Quiet Place* world?

**1444** WYR donate a $10 million inheritance to charitable causes or keep half and donate half to environmentally unsound organizations?

**1445** WYR be Doctor Who or Dr. Dolittle?

**1446** WYR be right but resented by others or wrong and constantly reminded of it by others?

**1447** WYR live in Amityville or Salem's Lot?

**1448** WYR be lonely on your own or lonely in a crowd?

**1449** WYR have Inspector Clouseau or Inspector Gadget solve your mystery?

**1450** WYR be a member of the Ghostbusters team or the X-Files team?

**1451** WYR die a horrible death or eat a part of your body to survive?

**1452** WYR be a cyborg or a Dalek?

**1453** WYR be haunted by the ghost of Billy the Kid or Bonnie Parker?

**1454** WYR be rich and mean or poor and kind?

**1455** WYR stay forever on Gilligan's Island or in Brigadoon?

**1456** WYR live in a world with no electricity or no animals?

**1457** WYR have MacGyver or Chuck Norris on your side in a food fight?

**1458** WYR have $5 million that must be spent within five days or have $1 million to do with as you please in five years' time?

**1459** WYR stick by the belief that honesty is the best policy or that nice guys finish last?

**1460** WYR be able to instantly overcome a fear or instantly read a book?

**1461** WYR know all things or have some things in life remain a mystery?

**1462** WYR become uglier as you age or dumber as you age?

**1463** WYR share an apartment with a neat freak or a slob?

**1464** WYR look better in photographs than you do in person or sound better on the phone than you do in person?

**1465** WYR never change your bedsheets or never eat your favorite brand of potato chips again?

**1466**  WYR accidentally spit on someone's face when talking or drop your phone into a toilet?

**1467**  WYR stink or have everybody else stink except you?

**1468**  WYR be able to blow bubbles out of your belly button or vomit a rainbow?

**1469**  WYR have chubby cheeks or fat fingers?

**1470**  WYR watch a movie with someone who keeps talking or someone who keeps rewinding?

**1471**  WYR have your parents embarrass you or be a disappointment to your parents?

**1472**  WYR listen to a ten-minute drum solo or a ten-minute banjo solo?

**1473**  WYR peel potatoes to feed 300 people or sort 600 socks into pairs?

**1474**  WYR get $1 every time someone said something good about you or every time someone thought something bad about you?

**1475**  WYR feel compelled to salute everyone you pass on the street or compelled to rap every time you speak?

**1476**  WYR sit in a wet chair or step into a deeper-than-anticipated puddle?

**1477**  WYR be caught dancing in your underwear or caught licking your plate?

**1478**  WYR drink apple juice that tastes like pee or drink pee that tastes like apple juice?

**1479**  WYR dance with someone who has no natural rhythm or sing with someone who is tone deaf?

**1480**  WYR have ugly toenails or hairy feet?

**1481**  WYR have a friend who never pays their share or a friend who keeps asking to borrow money?

**1482**  WYR be told you're too serious or you're too ridiculous?

**1483**  WYR read a book containing poor grammar or one with a weak plotline?

**1484** WYR forget to pack clean underwear or a change of footwear when traveling?

**1485** WYR have been an ancient king's food taster or be a modern-day dog food taster?

**1486** WYR eat buffalo wings or buffalo mozzarella?

**1487** WYR have a messenger owl or a messenger cheetah?

**1488** WYR be obese for the rest of your life or be hungry for the rest of your life?

**1489** WYR be a jock or a nerd?

**1490** WYR be unable to say any words beginning with D or any words beginning with R?

**1491** WYR knock out both front teeth in a bike accident or break both your wrists in a skateboard accident?

**1492** WYR be one of The Spiders from Mars or one of Buddy Holly's Crickets?

**1493** WYR hang out with Gonzo or Cookie Monster?

**1494** WYR have a night out with Miley Cyrus or Billie Ray Cyrus?

**1495** WYR be trained by Obi-Wan Kenobi or Mr. Miyagi?

**1496** WYR watch the original 1960s *Batman* TV series or the 1989 *Batman* movie?

**1497** WYR be paired with Rocky Balboa or John Matrix (*Commando*) in a three-legged race?

**1498** WYR do 1,000 sit-ups nonstop or 2,000 jumping jacks nonstop?

**1499** WYR wear wrinkled clothes or dirty shoes?

**1500** WYR maintain your ideal weight or always do what you say you're going to do?

**1501** WYR everyone in the world suddenly became much younger than you or much older than you?

**1502** WYR be roommates with Joey from *Friends* or Mork from *Mork and Mindy*?

**1503** WYR use a keyboard with the letters rubbed off or a phone with the numbers rubbed off?

**1504** WYR restaurant meals came with a free dessert or a free appetizer?

**1505** WYR wear a diving mask and snorkel or dinosaur-feet slippers?

**1506** WYR commute to work in a hovercraft or an ultralight plane?

**1507** WYR only be able to wear Crocs or only wear pajamas?

**1508** WYR shoot hoops with Michael Jordan or play a round of golf with Tiger Woods?

**1509** WYR sing like Freddie Mercury or play drums like Phil Collins?

**1510** WYR have been at Woodstock in 1969 or Live Aid in 1985?

**1511** WYR have twenty-two ducks or six goats?

**1512** WYR have private entry to Disney World or get a behind-the-scenes tour at Google?

**1513** WYR have free tickets to any baseball game for life or get paid $500,000 to never watch any baseball game ever again?

**1514** WYR be Genghis Khan or Atilla the Hun?

**1515** WYR kill off the baddie in your novel by having them fall under a steamroller or into a woodchipper?

**1516** WYR have your face in a painting or your body in a sculpture?

**1517** WYR not be able to use touch commands or not be able to use voice commands on your devices?

**1518** WYR have Godzilla or King Kong on your hockey team?

**1519** WYR kiss a frog or be kissed by a monkey?

**1520** WYR wake up in a *My Little Pony* world or a *Hunger Games* world?

**1521** WYR own up to making a mistake or own up to telling a lie?

**1522** WYR dress the way you did when you were thirteen years old or in the fashions of thirteen years ago?

1523　WYR never have a headache again or never eat jellybeans again?

1524　WYR hang out with Jabba the Hutt or someone who can only speak using quotes from movies?

1525　WYR wear a leotard and fanny pack or a Pierrot clown outfit complete with teardrop?

1526　WYR sing and dance "Greased Lightnin'" from *Grease* or "YMCA" by Village People on the hour every hour?

1527　WYR only watch Vin Diesel movies or Owen Wilson movies?

1528　WYR your eyes make the sound of camera shutters when you blink or sound like a steam train when you move?

1529　WYR face the wrath of Zeus or the wrath of Poseidon?

1530　WYR win $1,000,000 or have your friend win $3,000,000?

1531　WYR be a zombie slayer or a tooth fairy?

1532　WYR burp bubbles or sneeze confetti?

1533　WYR trick or treat?

1534　WYR be an Olympic athlete or a Hollywood actor?

1535　WYR never eat Taco Bell again or never wash your hands again?

1536　WYR have a day off like Ferris Bueller or an excellent adventure like Bill and Ted?

1537　WYR be hit with a frying pan, *Tom and Jerry*-style, or fall off cliffs, Wile E. Coyote-style?

1538　WYR have access to "Acme Corporation" devices or be able to set traps like Fred in Scooby-Doo?

1539　WYR sound like Kermit the Frog or Sylvester the Cat?

1540　WYR be deaf or blind?

1541　WYR be Paul McCartney or Mick Jagger?

1542　WYR be insane and know you're insane or insane and believe you're sane?

1543  WYR have been a passenger on the Hindenburg or on the Titanic?

1544  WYR have the A-Team or Charlie's Angels come to your rescue?

1545  WYR drive a fire truck or an ambulance?

1546  WYR have a lazy Susan on your table or a La-Z-Boy chair?

1547  WYR be able to crack your joints or lick your elbow?

1548  WYR be Joe 90 or Captain Scarlet?

1549  WYR travel at the speed of light or travel around the world in eighty days?

1550  WYR live in the world of Al Capone or the world of Bugsy Malone?

1551  WYR visit Area 51 or travel through the Bermuda Triangle?

1552  WYR have 200 horses or a vehicle with 200 horsepower?

1553  WYR bet everything you own on black or on red?

1554  WYR be featured on the front page of *The New York Times* or *Sports Illustrated*?

1555  WYR be a contestant on *Wheel of Fortune* or *Jeopardy*?

1556  WYR be part of Justin Bieber's entourage or Beyoncé's entourage?

1557  WYR time travel in a DeLorean (*Back to the Future)* or in a police box (*Doctor Who*)?

1558  WYR be James Bond or Jason Bourne?

1559  WYR have your fingers turn into hot dogs or your ears turn into donuts for an hour?

1560  WYR have a tapeworm or come face to face with a giant worm?

1561  WYR be a criminal living in the times of hanging or in the times of beheading by guillotine?

1562  WYR be in a globally famous band popular with kindergarten kids or be in an obscure rock band?

1563  WYR watch only movies directed by Steven Spielberg or by Quentin Tarantino?

**1564** WYR be a master computer programmer or a master craftsperson?

**1565** WYR be able to see The Beatles in concert or the Ramones in concert?

**1566** WYR dress like a rapper or dress like a rockabilly?

**1567** WYR hire Knight Rider or Magnum, P.I. to fight in your corner?

**1568** WYR have your house blown down by the big bad wolf or carried away by a twister?

**1569** WYR wear all denim or all plaid?

**1570** WYR have known Rosa Parks in the 1950s or Mahatma Gandhi in the 1920s?

**1571** WYR have an *Airwolf* helicopter or a *CHiPs* motorcycle?

**1572** WYR play *Space Invaders* or *Pacman*?

**1573** WYR go on a dinner date with Voldemort or Darth Vader?

**1574** WYR stare daggers at someone or have an all-out shouting match?

**1575** WYR have Captain Kirk or Captain Picard give you orders?

**1576** WYR live in a world without Velcro or a world without Post-It notes?

**1577** WYR be the CEO of a Fortune 500 company or the owner of a craft brewery?

**1578** WYR eat five cans of baked beans every day or fifteen Brussels sprouts every day?

**1579** WYR have an elephant step on your foot or a lion cub bite your hand?

**1580** WYR be one of the Goonies or one of the Spy Kids?

**1581** WYR be raised in a one-parent family or be an only child with both parents?

**1582** WYR wear a poncho every day for a week or never wear any item of clothing more than once?

**1583**  WYR ride on the flying luckdragon in *The NeverEnding Story* or in *Chitty Chitty Bang Bang*?

**1584**  WYR have a part in the 1950s movies *The Blob* or *Invasion of the Body Snatchers*?

**1585**  WYR never be able to say "please" or never be able to say "thank you"?

**1586**  WYR swim with otters or hang out with Fantastic Mr. Fox?

**1587**  WYR visit Timbuktu or Zootopia?

**1588**  WYR play cards with Beetlejuice or Gollum?

**1589**  WYR walk like Charlie Chaplin or John Wayne?

**1590**  WYR drive a Smart car or a Hummer?

**1591**  WYR shoot yourself in the hand with a nail gun or kneel down onto an exposed two-inch nail?

**1592**  WYR be wanted or needed?

**1593**  WYR go hard or go home?

**1594**  WYR live in your car for a week or move in with an elderly aunt for a month?

**1595**  WYR be on-trend or dare to be different and set your own style?

**1596**  WYR only be able to speak to ask a question or only be able to speak when asked a question?

**1597**  WYR be a city worker wearing a Stetson ten-gallon hat or a rancher wearing stylish sneakers?

**1598**  WYR be trapped in a sandstorm or caught in quicksand?

**1599**  WYR get a part in a stage play or on a TV soap opera?

**1600**  WYR run out of toothpaste or run out of deodorant?

**1601**  WYR know "the ways of the force" or know "the secret of Monkey Island"?

**1602**  WYR have a pocket watch or a grandfather clock?

**1603** WYR be the loudest talker in the room or wear the loudest outfit in the room?

**1604** WYR be Harry Styles's hairstylist or Britney Spears's hairstylist?

**1605** WYR eat your weight in snails or drink your weight in squid ink?

**1606** WYR listen to "Crazy Frog" or "Barbie Girl" on a loop?

**1607** WYR wear the fashions of ancient Rome or Victorian London?

**1608** WYR play Connect Four or Hungry Hungry Hippos?

**1609** WYR be a child star actor who fails as an adult actor or a one-hit wonder in the music industry?

**1610** WYR never hear the sound of chalk squeaking on a blackboard or the sound of slurping again?

**1611** WYR eat salad instead of Thanksgiving dinner or eat radishes instead of popcorn at the cinema?

**1612** WYR be the audience warm-up guy or the fat lady who sings at the end?

**1613** WYR be part of a firing squad or be a hangman?

**1614** WYR have a stomachache or have a sore throat?

**1615** WYR never have a dream come true or have your biggest dream *and* your worst nightmare come true?

**1616** WYR be a language teacher or a science teacher?

**1617** WYR be fit enough to run a marathon or climb Mount Everest?

**1618** WYR learn how to read again or learn how to walk again?

**1619** WYR eat nothing but cinnamon rolls for a week or only eat one cinnamon roll a year?

**1620** WYR visit a unicorn petting zoo or a dragon ride park?

**1621** WYR spend a weekend with a paranoid person or someone who has just been dumped?

**1622** WYR have a miniature Falabella horse or a miniature pot-bellied pig?

**1623** WYR never grate your finger on a cheese grater again or never burn your finger on toast again?

**1624** WYR eat mac and cheese with chopsticks or noodles with a spoon?

**1625** WYR live for a year without money or without electricity?

**1626** WYR have everything you touch turn to ice or turn to dust?

**1627** WYR be a boy mistaken for a girl or a girl mistaken for a boy?

**1628** WYR use mustard as toothpaste or toothpaste as cake frosting?

**1629** WYR not get a haircut for six months or get a buzz cut?

**1630** WYR have a sleepover with Wilma Flintstone or Marge Simpson?

**1631** WYR dress like Velma or Daphne from *Scooby-Doo*?

**1632** WYR be Olive, the Other Reindeer or Santa's Little Helper?

**1633** WYR give up potatoes or pasta?

**1634** WYR be able to make a sound like a grasshopper or light up like a glowworm?

**1635** WYR have all dogs try to attack you when they see you or all birds try to attack you when they see you?

**1636** WYR do the "Chicken Dance" or "Macarena" at every party you attend?

**1637** WYR be able to catch flies with your tongue like a frog or swivel your eyes like a chameleon?

**1638** WYR be Luke Skywalker or Flash Gordon?

**1639** WYR have a kitten climb up your leg or a puppy bite your toes?

**1640** WYR have two left hands or two left feet?

**1641** WYR fly with Amelia Earhart or Phileas Fogg?

**1642** WYR hang out with Peppa Pig or Big Bird?

**1643** WYR only be able to drink coffee at Starbucks or only be able to eat donuts at Dunkin' Donuts?

**1644** WYR slow down to walk with someone or have to jog to keep up with them?

**1645** WYR go caving or mountain climbing?

**1646** WYR eat cherry pie or cherry cake?

**1647** WYR pee your pants at a friend's party or pee in a swimming pool?

**1648** WYR have a physical job or take part in physical activities in your leisure time?

**1649** WYR go on a protest march or start an online petition?

**1650** WYR be in a relationship with someone ten years older or ten years younger than you?

**1651** WYR break a bone or chip a tooth?

**1652** WYR cut your own hair or have Edward Scissorhands cut your hair?

**1653** WYR have a wardrobe malfunction or show up wearing the same outfit as someone else?

**1654** WYR start a hashtag or share someone else's post?

**1655** WYR have food poisoning or get a cold sore?

**1656** WYR wear uncomfortable underwear or go commando?

**1657** WYR live in a cave or live in a tree house?

**1658** WYR be a hitchhiker or pick up a hitchhiker?

**1659** WYR accidentally break an expensive item at a house party or throw up over the host?

**1660** WYR be the person who gets seasick on a boat or be sitting next to the person who gets seasick?

**1661** WYR eat an entire pack of Oreos in one sitting or eat a whole pizza on your own?

**1662** WYR never be fired from your job or never be questioned by a police officer?

**1663** WYR have a part-time job in a shoe store or at Burger King?

**1664**  WYR use a gas station bathroom or pee on the side of the road?

**1665**  WYR blame a fart on a pet or an elderly relative in the room?

**1666**  WYR take part in a roller derby or a stock car race?

**1667**  WYR be nominated for an Oscar ten times and never win or win on your first nomination and never be nominated again?

**1668**  WYR be the only fairy that can't fly or the elf that's twice the size of the other elves?

**1669**  WYR be pranked with a whoopee cushion or with plastic wrap in the doorway?

**1670**  WYR have your phone ring at full volume in the cinema or in the library?

**1671**  WYR be a false alibi for a friend or let a friend be jailed for something they didn't do?

**1672**  WYR wear glasses all the time or contact lenses all the time?

**1673**  WYR be on the Nerf gun side or the Super Soaker side as battle commences?

**1674**  WYR watch the *Ghostbusters* remake or *The Lion King* remake?

**1675**  WYR get the highest score or make the longest word in a game of Scrabble?

**1676**  WYR play *Candy Crush* or Spin the Bottle?

**1677**  WYR ride to work on a bike with training wheels or on Heelys skate shoes?

**1678**  WYR sleep in the top bunk of bunk beds for a week or sleep in a hammock for a week?

**1679**  WYR walk into the wrong restroom or poop in a public restroom and find there's no toilet paper?

**1680**  WYR accidentally shart or throw up in your mouth and swallow it?

**1681**  WYR dip fries into a milkshake or have bananas with pickle?

**1682**  WYR miss a high five or forget the punchline of the joke you're telling?

1683 WYR change a diaper or have a baby be sick on you?

1684 WYR lie in a job interview or use a fake ID?

1685 WYR be a vegetarian with a meat-eating partner or a meat-eater with a vegetarian partner?

1686 WYR crop dust in an elevator or clog the toilet at a friend's house?

1687 WYR be an amazing painter or a brilliant mathematician?

1688 WYR never lose your phone again or never lose your keys again?

1689 WYR disappoint a family member or a friend?

1690 WYR sit on a public toilet seat or break the "five-second rule" when food drops onto the floor?

1691 WYR dye your hair and regret it or tell someone you love them and not mean it?

1692 WYR eat alligator or Spam?

1693 WYR eat a whole jar of jam every day for a month or eat everything in your fridge today?

1694 WYR pick a wedgie in public or sneeze messily into your hand in public?

1695 WYR brush your teeth with a hairbrush or comb your hair with a fork?

1696 WYR plant a tree or unveil a plaque?

1697 WYR touch an electric fence or get a static shock from a car door?

1698 WYR see Taylor Swift or Eminem in concert?

1699 WYR have chapped lips that never heal or terrible dandruff that can't be treated?

1700 WYR be a survivor in a *Terminator* (computer uprising) world or *Dawn of the Dead* (zombie apocalypse) world?

1701 WYR have takeout on Tuesday or a family meal on Friday?

1702 WYR instantly change the color of your hair or the length of your hair?

**1703** WYR have a *Star Trek*-style phaser or a *Men in Black*-style neuralyzer?

**1704** WYR crawl everywhere or butt shuffle everywhere?

**1705** WYR be a guitar-smashing rock star or smash your computer with a baseball bat for real?

**1706** WYR have a car with a top speed of 30 mph or be able to run at 40 mph with endless endurance?

**1707** WYR be Harrison Ford as Han Solo or Indiana Jones?

**1708** WYR have been the first person to reach the North Pole or the first person to climb Mount Everest?

**1709** WYR have skin like a coconut shell or skin like a pineapple?

**1710** WYR live in Downton Abbey or Winterfell Castle (*Game of Thrones*)?

**1711** WYR be caught kissing your reflection or kissing a photo of a celebrity?

**1712** WYR never be in a car accident or never be in handcuffs?

**1713** WYR steal pens from work or steal candy from a kid?

**1714** WYR miss a deadline or miss a payment?

**1715** WYR get up early to get a job done or stay up late to get a job done?

**1716** WYR vomit in a taxi or pee your pants in a taxi?

**1717** WYR know when you're going to die or how you're going to die?

**1718** WYR have unlimited sushi for life or unlimited tacos for life?

**1719** WYR accidentally break a piece of furniture by sitting on it or accidentally break a window?

**1720** WYR eat candy for dinner or survive on nothing but Dr. Pepper for a whole day?

**1721** WYR pretend to be in a music video or pretend to have your own cooking show?

**1722**  WYR be shouted at by a customer or by your boss?

**1723**  WYR break up with someone in public or have someone break up with you by text?

**1724**  WYR eat butter on its own or buffalo sauce on its own?

**1725**  WYR never pick a scab or never fart in a bath?

**1726**  WYR talk to yourself or talk to Alexa (Siri)?

**1727**  WYR be able to shed your skin like a snake or regrow a missing limb like a salamander?

**1728**  WYR share a water bottle with three friends or share a dip with a double dipper?

**1729**  WYR find a hair in your food or a fly in your drink?

**1730**  WYR have Thousand Island dressing on a salad or vinaigrette?

**1731**  WYR have your face pushed into a birthday cake or have your birthday cake explode when you cut it?

**1732**  WYR be baked like a cake or boiled like an egg?

**1733**  WYR have a mud bath or a dust bath?

**1734**  WYR eat food that has fallen on the ground or an old candy found in a pocket?

**1735**  WYR claim a cake by sticking your finger in it or lick the cream out of an Oreo and leave the cookies?

**1736**  WYR be blown over by the wind or knocked off your feet by a wave?

**1737**  WYR only eat sushi for a week or only eat Indian food for a week?

**1738**  WYR rock out to Green Day or bop to Katy Perry?

**1739**  WYR never get a speeding ticket or never get carded?

**1740**  WYR have one nipple or two belly buttons?

**1741**  WYR have a mustache drawn on your face when you're asleep or an L drawn on your forehead?

**1742** WYR get something stuck up your nose or in your ear?

**1743** WYR hide money under the mattress or in the closet?

**1744** WYR meet a mermaid or an elf?

**1745** WYR have been a teacher's pet or had a school pet?

**1746** WYR do your own catering at a house party or get caterers in?

**1747** WYR have been picked for the school's sports team or picked for the lead in the school musical?

**1748** WYR regret a haircut or regret a piercing?

**1749** WYR be able to drive stick shift or have a private limo?

**1750** WYR do a tandem bungee jump or a tandem skydive?

**1751** WYR dance on a table or slide down a bannister?

**1752** WYR know how to milk a cow or lasso a calf?

**1753** WYR eat food from a food truck or cook TV dinner at home?

**1754** WYR not be able to see any colors or have mild but constant tinnitus (ringing in the ears)?

**1755** WYR have constantly dry eyes or a constant runny nose?

**1756** WYR spend all day sitting or standing?

**1757** WYR listen to Johnny Cash or Johnny Rotten of the Sex Pistols?

**1758** WYR watch *Desperate Housewives* or *Real Housewives*?

**1759** WYR have a colonial-style house or a Tudor-style house?

**1760** WYR have a pool table room in your home or an outdoor swimming pool?

**1761** WYR have a day at the races (horse racing) or spectate at a polo tournament?

**1762** WYR know the history of every object you touched or be able to talk to animals?

**1763** WYR travel Route 66 on a Harley-Davidson or in a Ford Mustang?

**1764**  WYR cross Canada by train or cross Australia in an RV?

**1765**  WYR go to a monster truck rally or visit a mini golf center?

**1766**  WYR have a week-long vacation in Ireland or a long weekend in Hong Kong?

**1767**  WYR work on a production line or work in research?

**1768**  WYR be a physical therapist or a psychologist?

**1769**  WYR be given a head massage or a foot massage?

**1770**  WYR speak to an automated service or speak to a person?

**1771**  WYR have a salty snack with a beer or a sweet snack with a soda?

**1772**  WYR have a hi-tech security system or two large guard dogs?

**1773**  WYR have a large flower garden or a window-box vegetable garden?

**1774**  WYR be kept alive for years on life support or be allowed to die?

**1775**  WYR always grind coffee beans to make coffee or only drink instant coffee?

**1776**  WYR play charades or Pictionary?

**1777**  WYR only go to theme parties or only go to dinner parties?

**1778**  WYR smuggle candy into a movie theater or buy the biggest bucket of popcorn at the theater?

**1779**  WYR be forced to eat only spicy food or only incredibly bland food?

**1780**  WYR sleep in the nude or sleep without bed linen?

**1781**  WYR have a life-changing adventure or be able to stop time?

**1782**  WYR travel first class and stay in a budget hotel or travel budget class and stay in a five-star hotel?

**1783**  WYR only be able to listen to The Who albums or only be able to watch *Doctor Who* on TV?

**1784** WYR be responsible for the death of a child or for the deaths of three adults?

**1785** WYR have a pet jellyfish or a pet stick insect?

**1786** WYR be twelve inches tall or twelve feet tall?

**1787** WYR watch *Home Alone* or *National Lampoon's Christmas Vacation* on Christmas Eve every year?

**1788** WYR finish an entire jawbreaker or eat a whole box of Nerds in one sitting?

**1789** WYR meet the author of your favorite book or be able to meet a character from the book?

**1790** WYR go to jail for four years for something you didn't do or get away with something you did but live in fear of being caught?

**1791** WYR play video games for twelve hours nonstop or watch movies for twelve hours nonstop?

**1792** WYR it always rained on Sundays or it was always glorious weather on Mondays when you're back at work?

**1793** WYR walk into a post when texting or trip up a flight of stairs when texting?

**1794** WYR relax in a bubble bath or relax by a pool?

**1795** WYR only ever have one hairstyle and no bad hair days or have the option to try lots of different styles?

**1796** WYR never be sweaty again or never get dirty again?

**1797** WYR get free tickets to a theme park or a water park?

**1798** WYR be a Minion or an Oompa-Loompa?

**1799** WYR only eat McDonald's in a foreign country or try the local delicacies?

**1800** WYR wake up in Wonderland or Xanadu?

**1801** WYR lose your swimwear after diving into a pool or lose your shades over the side of a boat?

**1802** WYR be an extra in an Oscar-winning movie or the lead in a box office bomb?

**1803** WYR only be able to read the *Dork Diaries* series of books or the *Diary of a Wimpy Kid* series?

**1804** WYR have a crooked nose or a cauliflower ear from a sports injury?

**1805** WYR cook a meal blindfolded or eat a meal with your hands tied behind your back?

**1806** WYR army crawl everywhere or log roll everywhere?

**1807** WYR tie your shoelaces wearing mittens or send a text using only your nose?

**1808** WYR be able to balance a spoon on the end of your nose or touch your nose with your tongue?

**1809** WYR hold an ice cube in your hand until it melts or fill your mouth with ice cubes and wait until they melt?

**1810** WYR pop a balloon using your teeth or make an important phone call with a toffee in your mouth?

**1811** WYR be goosed or be given a wet willy?

**1812** WYR be hypnotized to walk around like a cat or like a catwalk model?

**1813** WYR answer the phone in a Mickey Mouse voice or a Bullwinkle voice?

**1814** WYR wear medieval jester shoes or traditional Dutch wooden shoes?

**1815** WYR be a Disney hero or a Disney villain?

**1816** WYR be a juggling acrobat or a parkour champion?

**1817** WYR be able to ride a unicycle or climb a rope using only your arms?

**1818** WYR be able to talk to and understand cats or dogs?

**1819** WYR be a skilled seamstress/tailor or have "a very particular set of skills" like Liam Neeson in *Taken*?

**1820** WYR chew on a raw clove of garlic or chug a cup of hot sauce?

**1821** WYR win a staring contest or an arm-wrestling match?

**1822** WYR be known as the life and soul of the party or the go-to person in an emergency?

**1823** WYR know how to build a house or know how to win at poker?

**1824** WYR dress in a burlap sack or wear a paper bag on your head?

**1825** WYR have an itch you can't scratch or be up poop creek without a paddle?

**1826** WYR go to work wearing one shoe for a day or wear one shoe and one sandal for a week?

**1827** WYR drink beer (soda) out of a friend's sneaker or eat potato chips out of a used ice hockey helmet?

**1828** WYR hang out with Crocodile Dundee or Conan the Barbarian?

**1829** WYR be a professional ballroom dancer or a professional window cleaner?

**1830** WYR live in a Manhattan penthouse or a Beverly Hills mansion?

**1831** WYR always be overdressed or always underdressed?

**1832** WYR be prone to dropping things or prone to forgetting things?

**1833** WYR be known by one name (mononymous) or have a hyphenated last name?

**1834** WYR get an animal-image tattoo or have a tattoo of someone's name?

**1835** WYR be a mad scientist like Doc Brown (*Back to the Future*) or a supervillain like Gru (*Despicable Me*)?

**1836** WYR eat dried fruit instead of fresh fruit or vegetable chips instead of fresh vegetables?

**1837** WYR take part in the "mannequin challenge" or the "ice bucket challenge"?

**1838** WYR have a secret family recipe or a family heirloom?

**1839** WYR take part in the "Cannonball Run" or the "Wacky Races"?

**1840** WYR have $25,000 in gold or in bitcoin?

**1841** WYR have seven sons or seven daughters?

**1842** WYR have a ninety percent chance of winning $90,000 or a fifty percent chance of winning $50 million?

**1843** WYR give up your car for a month or give up the internet for a week?

**1844** WYR have been best buddies with Albert Einstein or Stephen Hawking?

**1845** WYR own three homes or have $300,000 in the bank?

**1846** WYR be a TV or a TV remote control?

**1847** WYR be in a *War of the Worlds* world or a *Walking Dead* world?

**1848** WYR be an oil tycoon or a property magnate?

**1849** WYR be immune to physical pain or have no emotions?

**1850** WYR be a logical thinker or be considered a bit of a space cadet?

**1851** WYR have Ed Sheeran or Lewis Capaldi write a song about you?

**1852** WYR be lucky in love or talented in your career?

**1853** WYR be famous for pulling off an audacious heist or a daring jailbreak?

**1854** WYR be the record producer who turned down The Beatles or the publisher who rejected J.K. Rowling?

**1855** WYR be on a long car journey with a smartass or a dumbass?

**1856** WYR win a "World's Strongest . . ." title or a "World's Fastest . . ." title?

**1857** WYR be the second choice of your first love or be the first choice of your second love?

**1858** WYR be assimilated into the Borg (*Star Trek*) or have your brain transplanted into an animal form (Rocket Raccoon)?

**1859**  WYR cheat death or cheat on a partner?

**1860**  WYR socialize with mega-rich entrepreneurs or famous musicians?

**1861**  WYR love your face but not your body or love your body but not your face?

**1862**  WYR be the defense attorney for a guilty person or the prosecution against an innocent person?

**1863**  WYR share an office with a narcissist or a sociopath?

**1864**  WYR be malnourished or dehydrated?

**1865**  WYR have Morgan Freeman or Patrick Stewart narrate your life story?

**1866**  WYR only eat raw broccoli (never cooked) or cooked carrots (never raw)?

**1867**  WYR bring back the dire wolf or the saber-toothed cat?

**1868**  WYR Mark Zuckerberg or Oprah Winfrey became U.S. president?

**1869**  WYR be transported into the world of Oliver Twist or the world of Huckleberry Finn?

**1870**  WYR defend yourself with an electric hand whisk or a waffle iron?

**1871**  WYR wipe Valentine's Day or Groundhog Day from the calendar?

**1872**  WYR hire a sixteen-year-old babysitter or a seventy-six-year-old babysitter?

**1873**  WYR join the Avengers or the Justice League for a day?

**1874**  WYR live in a small apartment that's a five-minute walk from your workplace or a big house that's a thirty-minute drive away?

**1875**  WYR have been twenty-one in 1969 or twenty-one in 1989?

**1876**  WYR live in an apocalyptic world or a dystopian world?

**1877**  WYR spend time doing it yourself to save money or spend money on having someone else do it to save time?

**1878**  WYR take a pay cut to stay in your current job or cut your losses and look for another job?

**1879** WYR trade some of your looks to gain greater intelligence or trade some of your intelligence for better looks?

**1880** WYR choose truth or dare?

**1881** WYR vacation for a week in Alaska or a weekend in *Cancún*?

**1882** WYR take the blame to get your best friend out of trouble or take credit for something to get your worst enemy into trouble?

**1883** WYR dine in at your second favorite restaurant or get takeout from your favorite restaurant?

**1884** WYR own an elephant the size of a gerbil or a gerbil the size of an elephant?

**1885** WYR be a Transformer that turns into a Barbie convertible or a Barbie that turns into a dinosaur?

**1886** WYR increase the speed limit on rural U.S. highways to 80 mph or decrease the legal alcohol purchasing age to eighteen?

**1887** WYR hear the Beastie Boys singing lullabies or a K-pop band singing Slipknot songs?

**1888** WYR that money really did grow on trees or that wishes really were horses?

**1889** WYR be the Very Hungry Caterpillar or the Grouchy Ladybug?

**1890** WYR only be able to see one color or smell one smell?

**1891** WYR have bed sheets made of paper or carpets made of real grass?

**1892** WYR hear a growl behind you or a scream ahead of you when you're alone in the woods?

**1893** WYR be the creator of a new dance craze or a new toy craze?

**1894** WYR be head of product development with an awesome idea at Subway or Arby's?

**1895** WYR be a gladiator armed only with a fly swatter or a ninja warrior in squeaky clown shoes?

**1896** WYR have the power to cause chaos by transporting a furious elephant into any moment in history or by transporting a modern gadget?

**1897** WYR deal with snakes on a plane or birds in Bodega Bay (Hitchcock)?

**1898** WYR start a secret society or watch *The Secret Life of Pets*?

**1899** WYR have a giant TV screen in every room in your home or a high-fidelity multi-room sound system?

**1900** WYR have been one of the five mice that orbited the moon in 1972 or one of the Three Blind Mice?

**1901** WYR be able to change your name or choose your own nickname?

**1902** WYR be able to live someone else's life for fifteen minutes or read someone's thoughts for fifteen minutes?

**1903** WYR sing in front of an audience without music or dance in front of an audience without music?

**1904** WYR work Monday to Friday every week or Friday to Monday every week?

**1905** WYR be able to ask JFK three questions or Prince three questions?

**1906** WYR own a cat with a human face or a dog with human hands for paws?

**1907** WYR be tasked with redesigning your country's national flag or rewriting its national anthem?

**1908** WYR be Richard Dreyfuss's character in *Close Encounters of the Third Kind* or Will Smith's character in *Independence Day*?

**1909** WYR be a cartoon character from the 1960s or the 2000s?

**1910** WYR live in a world where tarantulas or foxes are the most common pet?

**1911** WYR have a fear of a duck watching you (anatidaephobia) or fear of the color yellow (xanthophobia)?

**1912** WYR have a window in your toaster to see when the toast is done or translucent skin to see your muscles working?

**1913** WYR be able to revive plants with your tears or kill weeds with your laughter?

**1914** WYR merge Mousetrap and Clue or Exploding Kittens and Old Maid into a new game?

**1915** WYR make freeze dance (musical statues) or red light, green light an Olympic sport?

**1916** WYR have an intergalactic spaceship or a *ThunderCats* ThunderTank?

**1917** WYR fill your home interior with festive decorations or cover the exterior in lights that can be seen from space?

**1918** WYR make it customary to say "May the force be with you" or "Pikachu" when someone sneezes?

**1919** WYR have the power to rename cities or rename brands?

**1920** WYR be born again in a different country or born again as the opposite sex?

**1921** WYR be armed with a banjo or an egg whisk in a zombie attack?

**1922** WYR be stranded on an island like Tom Hanks in *Castaway* or stranded on Mars like Matt Damon in *The Martian*?

**1923** WYR be named after a model of car or a household cleaning product?

**1924** WYR be caught dancing with a mop or singing with a banana microphone?

**1925** WYR switch bodies with a raccoon or a dolphin?

**1926** WYR go to the mall wearing Disney slippers or go to a nightclub wearing a beanie hat?

**1927** WYR have every sock you've ever lost appear all at once in your bedroom or every lost pet in your city?

**1928** WYR be able to give people ridiculous phobias for an hour or cure people of their phobias forever?

**1929** WYR only be able to listen to boy bands or female solo artists?

**1930** WYR work behind the scenes at The White House or work behind the scenes in Hollywood?

**1931** WYR rap everything you say or play air guitar to all the music you hear?

**1932** WYR be able to custom-make your ideal partner or your ideal family?

**1933** WYR hear the ground complaining when you walk on it or your car complaining when you drive badly?

**1934** WYR live in a castle in the clouds or on a magical island in a distant sea?

**1935** WYR be the first to discover the lost city of Atlantis or the lost city of El Dorado?

**1936** WYR animals walked upright for a day or humans walked on all-fours for a day?

**1937** WYR spend a day as Robinson Crusoe or Lemuel Gulliver (*Gulliver's Travels*)?

**1938** WYR climb every mountain or ford every stream?

**1939** WYR have freckles on your nose or a dimple on your chin?

**1940** WYR spend the day with Dora the Explorer or Curious George?

**1941** WYR sound like a pig or move like a baboon?

**1942** WYR be accused of being a spendthrift or a miser?

**1943** WYR win an overnight stay in a luxurious yurt or an ice hotel?

**1944** WYR laugh like a hyena or sound like a donkey when you laugh?

**1945** WYR meet a dinosaur or an alien?

**1946** WYR have tea with Charles Dickens or Beatrix Potter?

**1947** WYR never get lost or never lose your balance?

**1948** WYR play volleyball on the beach or Frisbee in the park?

**1949** WYR reveal your deepest fear or your secret crush?

**1950** WYR lick the floor or lick food retrieved from a trash can?

**1951** WYR be the opposite sex for a month or work the night shift for a month?

**1952** WYR be caught sucking your thumb or sleeping with a stuffed toy?

**1953** WYR hurt someone by telling a lie or by saying something mean?

**1954** WYR be a crack shot with a peashooter or a slingshot?

**1955** WYR be able to erase an ugly photo of you or something embarrassing you did from existence?

**1956** WYR wipe your nose on your sleeve or do a "farmer's blow" without a tissue?

**1957** WYR do four cartwheels to save your life or do the worm across the floor?

**1958** WYR shower with your clothes on or go swimming with your clothes on?

**1959** WYR sing and act through your day as if in an opera or sing and dance as if in a Broadway musical?

**1960** WYR have your lifetime experiences converted into a movie to watch whenever you want to remember them or have your life turned into a book that can be read by anyone?

**1961** WYR keep a smile on your face all day or get through a day without laughing?

**1962** WYR wash your hair with laundry detergent or wash your clothes with shampoo?

**1963** WYR never lose your memory or never lose your eyesight?

**1964** WYR have your most disgusting (and secret) habit discovered or be arrested by police and taken in for questioning?

**1965** WYR have a joke backfire on you or be tickled for a minute?

**1966** WYR hold a live insect in your mouth for ten seconds or have rats walk over you for ten seconds?

**1967** WYR sell something you know is slightly broken or serve up a meal you know doesn't taste great?

**1968**  WYR be able to spin a hula hoop for three minutes or juggle three eggs for a minute?

**1969**  WYR have to floss or do the running man dance move every time you hit the dance floor?

**1970**  WYR try to open a can of cola or a bag of potato chips without using your hands?

**1971**  WYR never feel envy again or never feel vengeful again?

**1972**  WYR have head lice or eczema?

**1973**  WYR find a skunk in your bed or a goose in your shower?

**1974**  WYR switch socks with the person on your left or switch tops with the person on your right?

**1975**  WYR listen to "Let It Go" from *Frozen* or "A Whole New World" from *Aladdin* for a whole day?

**1976**  WYR join a monkey grooming session or have an oxpecker bird clean through your hair?

**1977**  WYR eat a *Scooby-Doo*-style stacked sandwich or a torpedo sandwich?

**1978**  WYR have the mark of Simba or the scar of Harry Potter?

**1979**  WYR have all your clothes fit perfectly or have the most comfortable pillow, blankets, and sheets in existence?

**1980**  WYR take part in a twenty-four-hour dance-a-thon or a twenty-four-hour cook-a-thon?

**1981**  WYR permanently ban drunk drivers from driving again or increase jail time and fines?

**1982**  WYR survive on canned baked beans or Pop-Tarts?

**1983**  WYR be considered vain or plain?

**1984**  WYR put relationships over career or put your career first?

**1985**  WYR be considered aggressive or a pushover?

**1986**  WYR eat fish heads or eat fish food?

**1987** WYR get your toe stuck in a faucet or get locked out of your hotel room in your underwear?

**1988** WYR have hay fever or cabin fever?

**1989** WYR never learn how to drive or never learn how to shop online?

**1990** WYR step on an ant nest or agitate a beehive?

**1991** WYR have flour or wet sponges thrown at you?

**1992** WYR wear socks as gloves or oven gloves as a scarf?

**1993** WYR accidentally swallow mouthwash or get shampoo in your eyes?

**1994** WYR know how to pick a lock or how to hotwire a car?

**1995** WYR win a twerking contest or a karaoke contest?

**1996** WYR eat a kiwi fruit without peeling it or a fish without skinning it?

**1997** WYR feel free or safe?

**1998** WYR be challenged to a dance-off or a sing-off?

**1999** WYR be a member of your favorite band for a day or be transported into your favorite game for a day?

**2000** WYR have nine lives like a cat or live the life of Riley?

**2001** WYR be a world-class cage-fighter or a world-class wrestler?

**2002** WYR only check your social networks once a day in the morning or once a day in the evening?

**2003** WYR live a two-hour drive from open countryside or two hundred miles away from the beach?

**2004** WYR never be able to talk to anyone again or never be able to touch anyone again?

**2005** WYR work in waste disposal or bomb disposal?

**2006** WYR be transported into a game of *Pac-Man* as a ghost or into a game of *Space Invaders* as a bonus point mystery ship?

**2007** WYR slip and fall in a puddle of vomit or get sprayed by a skunk?

**2008** WYR vacation for a week in Westeros or a week in Narnia?

**2009** WYR be able to impersonate every Hollywood celebrity or be a look-alike for one?

**2010** WYR race on foot like Liddell and Abrahams in *Chariots of Fire* or race in a chariot like Ben-Hur?

**2011** WYR devote a year to searching for the Loch Ness Monster or searching for Sasquatch?

**2012** WYR be Aladdin or Ali Baba?

**2013** WYR live a hermit's life or be the life and soul of every party?

**2014** WYR have telescopic legs like Inspector Gadget or extendable arms like Mr. Tickle?

**2015** WYR see the creation of the universe or the end of the universe?

**2016** WYR avoid really big spiders or really fast spiders?

**2017** WYR lack imagination or lack subtlety?

**2018** WYR eat oxtail soup or beef tongue sandwiches?

**2019** WYR have one three-week-long vacation or three one-week-long vacations each year?

**2020** WYR eat a handful of hair or drink a cup of spit?

**2021** WYR go back in time and prevent WWII or 9/11?

**2022** WYR have narcolepsy (involuntary sleep episodes) or insomnia?

**2023** WYR only be able to eat green vegetables or red fruit?

**2024** WYR have to pay cash for all purchases over $100 or pay by credit card for purchases under $5?

**2025** WYR only eat ice cream in a cone or in a cup?

**2026** WYR only wear pullover hoodies or zip-up hoodies?

**2027** WYR be a solo singer with an acoustic guitar or the bass guitarist in a rock band?

**2028** WYR have bacon and eggs or a stack of pancakes for breakfast?

**2029** WYR go shopping for a new laptop or new shoes?

**2030** WYR be able to bake your own cakes or make your own candles?

**2031** WYR only be able to use snail mail or an old-fashioned non-cordless landline phone?

**2032** WYR never have dip with chips again or never have sauce with wings again?

**2033** WYR be prepared like a Boy Scout or be prepared to wing it?

**2034** WYR eat only pizza for a year or eat no pizza for a year?

**2035** WYR go lake fishing or eat fish and chips?

**2036** WYR wear a fur hat or snakeskin boots?

**2037** WYR wear clothes with patches or wear an eyepatch?

**2038** WYR have a helper monkey or a helper robot?

**2039** WYR swallow a quarter or butt-dial someone and have them hear what they shouldn't?

**2040** WYR watch *The Nightmare Before Christmas* or *A Nightmare on Elm Street*?

**2041** WYR be able to clear the world's oceans of plastic or save the rainforests?

**2042** WYR be able to answer the question of where Cotton-Eyed Joe came from or know where he went?

**2043** WYR wake up in a *Mad Max* world or the world of *Waterworld*?

**2044** WYR live with a dog that snores loudly or a partner who talks in their sleep?

**2045** WYR lose a day of your life every time you swear or every time you say something mean?

**2046** WYR be ding-dong ditched frequently or have your house toilet papered once?

**2047** WYR drink salad dressing out of the bottle or eat a lemon?

**2048** WYR hang out with the first person you ever had a crush on or the first person you ever dated?

**2049** WYR it was legal to be married to more than one person or illegal to have more than four children?

**2050** WYR be proactive or procrastinate?

**2051** WYR wear the fashions your parents wore as teenagers or the fashions your grandparents wore?

**2052** WYR have a part in a slasher movie or a disaster movie?

**2053** WYR get your tongue stuck to a frozen pole or get a wasp sting on your tongue?

**2054** WYR be the eager beaver or the lazy hound dog?

**2055** WYR be able to do a split or do a backflip?

**2056** WYR yodel in the Swiss Alps or beat on jungle drums in remote Africa?

**2057** WYR have free internet for life or free food for life?

**2058** WYR give a colleague a piggyback around your workplace for a day or be given piggybacks all day?

**2059** WYR eat a banana without peeling it or swallow gum?

**2060** WYR be a skilled whistler or a skilled spoons player?

**2061** WYR be "like a rhinestone cowboy" or "just like Jesse James"?

**2062** WYR have bad breath or smelly feet?

**2063** WYR have eyes that can film everything or ears that can record all sound?

**2064** WYR paint a picture or paint a garden fence?

**2065** WYR switch places with a spider or a mouse?

**2066** WYR live in a yellow submarine or in a big yellow taxi?

**2067** WYR have three eyes or a tail?

**2068** WYR be trapped in a room with walls moving in or tied to a post with water levels rising?

**2069** WYR wake up to a snake or a bear in your bedroom?

**2070** WYR have your car written off in a car crash or lose all your files in a computer crash?

**2071** WYR find $50 or be hugged?

**2072** WYR live in a country with a low cost of living but horrible weather or live in a country with a high cost of living and amazing weather?

**2073** WYR be a world-renowned photographer or a world-renowned animal trainer?

**2074** WYR feel brave or feel smart?

**2075** WYR share everything in your life with others or keep it all to yourself?

**2076** WYR understand how animals communicate or the laws of quantum mechanics?

**2077** WYR be able to successfully grow anything you want in the yard or be an accomplished classical musician?

**2078** WYR be a passenger in Toad of Toad Hall's motorcar (*The Wind in the Willows*) or Cruella de Vil's car (*101 Dalmatians*)?

**2079** WYR know the muffin man or know the way to San Jose?

**2080** WYR tell a stranger their underwear was showing or look the other way?

**2081** WYR fix the hole in the ozone layer or save the Great Barrier Reef?

**2082** WYR have money and no love or love and no money?

**2083** WYR have great wisdom or good health?

**2084** WYR be invited to tea with Queen Elizabeth II or the Dalai Lama?

**2085** WYR marry a poor person from your culture or a rich person from a different culture?

**2086** WYR cuddle a baby penguin or a baby panda?

3000 WYR QUESTIONS ABOUT ME

**2087** WYR be able to do ten pull-ups or cook pulled pork to die for?

**2088** WYR eat Sour Patch Kids or Swedish Fish?

**2089** WYR play Wiffle ball or foosball?

**2090** WYR everyone had to get married at the age of twenty-one or thirty-one?

**2091** WYR save Beyoncé or Rihanna from drowning, if you could save only one?

**2092** WYR be able to touch your toes without bending your knees or rub your tummy and pat your head?

**2093** WYR have no nose or no ears?

**2094** WYR be woken up by an air horn every morning or do a four-mile run on waking every morning?

**2095** WYR only eat ninety-five-percent cocoa dark chocolate or only eat white chocolate?

**2096** WYR meet a mini hippo or a giant wasp?

**2097** WYR argue that a tomato is a fruit or a vegetable?

**2098** WYR ban hairstyling products or foods containing garlic?

**2099** WYR bring back Tupac or Whitney Houston?

**2100** WYR be the apple of someone's eye or be someone with a finger in every pie?

**2101** WYR live in the world as it is today or live in the world as it was a hundred years ago?

**2102** WYR have met Ziggy Stardust or Zig Ziglar?

**2103** WYR work alone in the day or work with colleagues on the night shift?

**2104** WYR be in a marching band or be a rubber band?

**2105** WYR eat only nutritious meals prepared for you (no snacking) or eat whatever you crave at any time?

2106 WYR ask a loaded question or shoot from the hip when answering a question?

2107 WYR jump on the bandwagon or jump ship?

2108 WYR read the *Goosebumps* books or watch the *Are You Afraid of the Dark?* TV series?

2109 WYR train King Arthur's knights or Robin Hood's merry men to become a dance troupe?

2110 WYR let sleeping dogs lie or let the cat out of the bag?

2111 WYR only be able to take photos or shoot videos?

2112 WYR drink warm soda or eat cold curry?

2113 WYR see a pig that can fly or a fish that can ride a bicycle?

2114 WYR have a life-size candy cane or a life-size gummy bear?

2115 WYR be a skilled architect or a skilled graphic designer?

2116 WYR eat three square meals a day or five smaller meals a day?

2117 WYR go gray naturally as you age or dye your hair to cover gray as you age?

2118 WYR relax in sweatpants or in shorts?

2119 WYR only eat chocolate or only eat Haribos?

2120 WYR eat breakfast in a sunporch or drink sundowners out on a deck?

2121 WYR visit a book festival or an art festival?

2122 WYR go ghost hunting or storm chasing?

2123 WYR be part of the real CSI or the real FBI?

2124 WYR never have less than fifty percent charge on your phone or always have $50 in your pocket?

2125 WYR be a sheepdog or a mountain rescue dog?

2126 WYR have super-sharp reflexes or be super-flexible?

**2127** WYR own an ostentatious home or an ostentatious car?

**2128** WYR wear entirely neon pink or entirely plaid?

**2129** WYR have fine, straight hair or thick, curly hair?

**2130** WYR be a lifeguard or a Coast Guard "surfman"?

**2131** WYR have whatever you are thinking to appear above your head for everyone to see or have absolutely everything you do livestreamed for anyone to see?

**2132** WYR read a book by William Faulkner or Ernest Hemingway?

**2133** WYR be hated or be a hater?

**2134** WYR be in a long-distance relationship or be married to someone in the military?

**2135** WYR be a salsa dancer or a Broadway dancer?

**2136** WYR be a prom queen/king or valedictorian?

**2137** WYR be rich and famous or just rich?

**2138** WYR be sophisticated and aloof or be the boy/girl next door and gregarious?

**2139** WYR learn to communicate using Morse code or semaphore flag signals?

**2140** WYR have breakfast in bed or breakfast at Tiffany's?

**2141** WYR eat green apples or red grapes?

**2142** WYR go dancing or watch professional dancers perform?

**2143** WYR go without your phone or go without food for two days?

**2144** WYR have lunch with a friend or dinner with a colleague?

**2145** WYR study in your spare time over six months or go on a two-week intensive study course?

**2146** WYR play dominoes or eat Domino's?

**2147** WYR be the child of celebrity parents or have a famous sibling?

2148  WYR be born into a family that's feared (like Corleone) or have a sibling who is on death row?

2149  WYR be an identical twin or be a fraternal twin?

2150  WYR have a DJ or a live band at your party?

2151  WYR hang out with Justin Timberlake or Justin Chambers?

2152  WYR lose your heart to a starship trooper or leave your heart in San Francisco?

2153  WYR be a legendary adventurer or a legendary performer?

2154  WYR go sugar-free or gluten-free?

2155  WYR stay in bed all day or stay awake all night?

2156  WYR eat a pigeon or eat a guinea pig?

2157  WYR move to a new city or town every week or never be able to leave the city or town you were born in?

2158  WYR camp for a night with a stranger or camp for a night alone?

2159  WYR work for an angry boss or work in an environment that makes you angry?

2160  WYR save an antique painting or your favorite shoes from a fire?

2161  WYR be able to undo every mistake you ever made or never make another mistake going forward?

2162  WYR have charisma or great hair?

2163  WYR be alone on Valentine's Day or alone on New Year's Eve?

2164  WYR have a cut on your lip or a canker sore on your tongue?

2165  WYR be blackmailed or wear chain mail?

2166  WYR have a parrot that talks all day or a cat that yowls at night?

2167  WYR be held hostage for six months or go into hiding for six months?

2168  WYR rest in bed for twenty days or have to visit the hospital for treatment every day for twenty days?

**2169** WYR be surrounded by people who brag nonstop about their great life or people who moan nonstop about their unfair life?

**2170** WYR do an outdoor job in pouring rain or under a baking hot sun?

**2171** WYR be happy like a pig in muck or happy like a dog with two tails?

**2172** WYR pull out one of your own teeth or stitch up your own arm?

**2173** WYR sleepwalk in public wearing SpongeBob pajamas or One Direction pajamas?

**2174** WYR have a day out on a motorboat or a sightseeing trip in a helicopter?

**2175** WYR eat an orange or drink orange juice?

**2176** WYR lose all the photographs you've taken this year or all the photographs of you in your childhood?

**2177** WYR have four arms or two mouths?

**2178** WYR be able to wash yourself like a cat or dry yourself like a dog?

**2179** WYR live without the internet or without AC and heating?

**2180** WYR have gum stuck on your shoe or a hole in the sole of your shoe?

**2181** WYR have a puppy pee on you or a bird poop on you?

**2182** WYR be Optimus Prime or Bumblebee?

**2183** WYR a cat had kittens in your bed or a hen laid eggs in your bed?

**2184** WYR find a cockroach in your shoe as you put it on or in your pocket as you put your hand in?

**2185** WYR be able to turn yourself into a bat or into a mouse?

**2186** WYR share a cab with someone who has bad breath or someone with body odor?

**2187** WYR meet "the crooked man who walked a crooked mile" or "this old man who came rolling home"?

**2188** WYR meet the real Easter bunny or the real Santa?

**2189** WYR have hairs grow on the palms of your hands or on the outside of your ears?

**2190** WYR be able to read lips or know sign language?

**2191** WYR fall out of bed or fall off a bench?

**2192** WYR end racism or end sexism?

**2193** WYR plunge into ice-cold water or chug a glass of ice-cold water?

**2194** WYR have met Judy Garland or James Dean?

**2195** WYR lose the last piece of your 2,000-piece jigsaw or lose a card from your deck?

**2196** WYR eat only baby food for a day or watch *Blue's Clues* for an entire day?

**2197** WYR spend a night in the hospital or in jail?

**2198** WYR put candy on a pizza or dip chips in chocolate sauce?

**2199** WYR never play your favorite sport again or lose whenever you play?

**2200** WYR be seen driving over a curb or reversing into a mailbox?

**2201** WYR get a ten-minute answer whenever you ask "How are you?" or hear everything that's said with a ten-second delay?

**2202** WYR have a completely automated home or a self-driving car?

**2203** WYR find proof that there is a parallel universe or find proof that Big Foot is real?

**2204** WYR be blocked by someone on social media or be ghosted?

**2205** WYR pretend not to be home when your doorbell rings or reply to a text pretending to be someone else?

**2206** WYR break the law or break both your arms?

**2207** WYR cry for no reason or laugh for no reason?

**2208** WYR be a hip-hop superstar or hula hoop superstar?

**2209** WYR only be able to eat out of a bowl (no plates) or only be able to drink out of a mug?

**2210** WYR have met Anne Frank or Victor Frankenstein?

**2211** WYR be a fluffy rug on a floor or a delicate tapestry on a wall?

**2212** WYR have an overly possessive partner or an overly needy pet?

**2213** WYR be a roofer with a fear of heights or a coal miner with a fear of small spaces?

**2214** WYR be a bee in *Bee Movie* or an ant in *Antz*?

**2215** WYR have a photo album or a scrapbook?

**2216** WYR have a romantic dinner or a romantic slow dance?

**2217** WYR eat dry toast or dry crackers?

**2218** WYR be a cat with red eyes or a snake with a green tongue?

**2219** WYR be transported into a medieval banquet or a Roman feast?

**2220** WYR drink tequila with a worm in it or a "Sourtoe Cocktail" with a mummified toe in it?

**2221** WYR meet a shark in the dark or find a snake in your cake?

**2222** WYR wear a grass skirt to work or snow boots to the beach?

**2223** WYR have a traditional wedding or get married in Las Vegas?

**2224** WYR only need to sleep for one night each week or only need to eat one meal each week?

**2225** WYR be able to complete a one-week project in one day or complete two one-week projects in one week?

**2226** WYR be a bounty hunter or a bargain hunter?

**2227** WYR work as an apple picker or a strawberry picker?

**2228** WYR wear a neck brace for a month or have braces on your teeth for two months?

**2229** WYR your birthday coincided with a sibling's birthday or was on Christmas day?

**2230** WYR be on the outside looking in or be an outlier?

**2231** WYR only be able to read the first half of any book or watch the second half of any movie?

**2232** WYR ask a question no one wants to answer or give an answer no one wants to hear?

**2233** WYR sound like Donald Duck or say everything in the style of a wrestling announcer?

**2234** WYR decorate your home all in red or wear only red?

**2235** WYR be able to change the way your hair parts or change the shape of your eyebrows at will?

**2236** WYR have the Darth Vader theme play whenever you walk or leave a trail of glitter wherever you walk?

**2237** WYR be limited to Barbie's (G.I. Joe's) range of movement or stutter over your words like Porky Pig?

**2238** WYR have hair made of bendy straws or spaghetti?

**2239** WYR wear clothes made of newspaper or wear shoes made of banana peels?

**2240** WYR be a magnet to lint or have squirrels sneakily follow you wherever you go?

**2241** WYR make the sound of a bowling strike every time you stand up or a gong strike every time you sit down?

**2242** WYR your hair turned green in direct sunlight or your skin turned green when wet?

**2243** WYR have a job on an assembly line or a supermarket checkout?

**2244** WYR use sour cream-and-chive-scented shampoo or cheese-and-onion-scented deodorant?

**2245** WYR wear a sombrero or 1970s Elton John-style glasses every day for a week?

**2246** WYR have the power to instantly summon an elevator or instantly hail a cab?

**2247** WYR be able to change the length of your hair by pushing your belly button or have a prehensile ponytail?

**2248** WYR dive into a pool of pudding or a pool of Skittles?

**2249** WYR be able to sharpen pencils in your nostril or use your nose as an eraser?

**2250** WYR let the dogs out or walk the dinosaur?

**2251** WYR have glow-in-the-dark knees or elbows that can bend both ways?

**2252** WYR eat meatloaf or go to a Meatloaf concert?

**2253** WYR be chased by hyenas or hippos?

**2254** WYR find a live maggot after biting into a Milky Way or floating in your breakfast cereal milk?

**2255** WYR be on a long bus journey with twenty Elvis impersonators or twenty mime artists?

**2256** WYR settle an argument with a break-dancing contest or a bake-off?

**2257** WYR have to interpret an important message through a mime artist or an interpretive dancer?

**2258** WYR it rained raisins or snowed flaked almonds for a day?

**2259** WYR be able to adjust your height by twiddling your earlobe or change your hairstyle by pushing your nose?

**2260** WYR have paws instead of hands or hooves instead of feet?

**2261** WYR have the voice of Lewis Capaldi or the driving ability of Lewis Hamilton?

**2262** WYR be a master diorama maker or a master miniature golf course designer?

**2263** WYR have been a soldier at Custer's Last Stand or the Battle of the Alamo?

**2264** WYR know when to hold them and when to fold them or when to walk away and when to run (Kenny Rogers)?

2265 WYR be the Metro-Goldwyn-Mayer roaring lion or the Pixar hopping lamp?

2266 WYR sleep hanging upside down like a bat or sleep standing up like a giraffe?

2267 WYR be able to pop popcorn by holding it in your hands or cook pizzas with your eyes?

2268 WYR feel compelled to follow everything you say with an evil laugh or begin every sentence with "Simon says . . ."?

2269 WYR suddenly be elected a Governor or suddenly become a CEO of a Foturne 500 company?

2270 WYR have a compulsion to say "Kibbles" every time you blink or blurt out "Size of a whale!" at random intervals?

2271 WYR forget how to get dressed once a year or lose the ability to understand English for a day?

2272 WYR tell people you come from a galaxy far, far away or you come from a land that time forgot?

2273 WYR be stuck on a desert island with a basketball or a Rubik's Cube?

2274 WYR have an extreme phobia of trees and flowers or of people named after trees and flowers?

2275 WYR have your strength determined by the length of your hair or your intelligence by the length of your fingers?

2276 WYR be able to play your fingers like panpipes or your thighs like bongos?

2277 WYR sneeze uncontrollably every time you see a cat or itch uncontrollably every time you see a dog?

2278 WYR wear a Carmen Miranda-style fruit hat or a Lady Gaga-inspired meat outfit to work?

2279 WYR be a tealight on a harbor or a floodlight on a sports field?

2280 WYR have an interchangeable Lego head or be Mr. Potato Head?

2281 WYR sleepwalk and wake up on a train to New Orleans or wake up on an Ireland-bound boat?

**2282** WYR sound like Arnold Schwarzenegger or Sylvester Stallone?

**2283** WYR be able to choose the weather each day or choose how many hours you spend at work each day?

**2284** WYR survive on moon pies or whoopie pies?

**2285** WYR be on the trail of the lonesome pine or following the yellow brick road?

**2286** WYR have extreme flatulence for a day or wear an outfit knitted by your grandma?

**2287** WYR know how to play the piccolo or paint like Picasso?

**2288** WYR be able to style your hair by thinking about it or wash and dry your clothes by dancing around them?

**2289** WYR be a traditional witch riding a broomstick or a thoroughly modern witch riding a vacuum cleaner?

**2290** WYR be double-jointed or have an unlimited supply of Double Dip (Fun Dip) candy?

**2291** WYR be the undisputed tiddlywinks champion or pick-up sticks champion?

**2292** WYR sing the full version of your national anthem or recite the times tables up to twelve every morning?

**2293** WYR have Captain Kirk or Captain Han Solo on your tag team?

**2294** WYR be the world's greatest hippity-hopper or world's greatest chair-balancer?

**2295** WYR be the author of *101 Things to Do with a Stick* or *101 Meals to Make with Kale*?

**2296** WYR be the chicken that crossed the road or the duck that walked into a bar?

**2297** WYR be a computer mouse or a bug in the system?

**2298** WYR have a tiger in your tank or an earworm song in your head?

**2299** WYR be a pampered puss or a purse puppy?

**2300** WYR win the Nobel Prize in Physics or be a noble knight with a trusty steed?

**2301** WYR be Big Ben or Ben Cohen of Ben & Jerry's?

**2302** WYR be related to George Washington or Beyonce?

**2303** WYR have lunch with Charo or go water-skiing with Robert Redford?

**2304** WYR have a rabbit's foot lucky charm or eat Lucky Charms every day for breakfast?

**2305** WYR have the original Ghostbusters' Ecto-1 or the Blues Brothers' Bluesmobile?

**2306** WYR ride the wall of death or ride on the roof of a train across India?

**2307** WYR be locked overnight in a museum or an amusement park?

**2308** WYR have been one of Queen Elizabeth I's scullery maids or a Victorian chimney sweep?

**2309** WYR be haunted by the sound of a rustling chip packet or the smell of rotisserie chicken?

**2310** WYR be tasked with finding a needle in a haystack or finding a white cat in a snowstorm?

**2311** WYR find Nemo or find Waldo?

**2312** WYR be a storm in a teacup or be the eye of a storm?

**2313** WYR be able to magically transform into a crow or be Russell Crowe in *Gladiator*?

**2314** WYR be a mad scientist's guinea pig or live in a *Mad Max* world?

**2315** WYR be the "man with the golden gun" or "the man from Del Monte"?

**2316** WYR be "ready for this jelly" or "too sexy for your shirt"?

**2317** WYR give up peanut butter or give up two hours of sleep each night?

**2318** WYR enter an Elvis impersonator contest or the rock-paper-scissors world championships?

**2319** WYR ride in a pelican's beak or a kangaroo's pouch?

**2320** WYR have free Wi-Fi for a year or free Amazon Prime for life?

**2321** WYR have three wheels on your wagon or be three sheets to the wind?

**2322** WYR have a childhood scar from falling out of a tree or an adult scar from falling out of a tree?

**2323** WYR have someone else blow out your birthday candles or have someone steal your thunder?

**2324** WYR be an expert at guessing a song from its intro or be an expert at playing song intros on a piano?

**2325** WYR forget where you parked your car or accidently get into the wrong car?

**2326** WYR be one person's favorite person or be a fan favorite?

**2327** WYR yodel to save your life or tap dance to save your life?

**2328** WYR listen to the sound of a breeze in the trees or bacon sizzling?

**2329** WYR bring back 1970s striped tube socks or 1980s leg warmers?

**2330** WYR have your eye on the prize or play it by ear?

**2331** WYR win the lottery and die the next day or get a free ride when you've already paid?

**2332** WYR spend a rainy afternoon playing Uno with family or playing *Animal Crossing* alone?

**2333** WYR re-read a book or re-watch a movie?

**2334** WYR only be able to wash your hair three times a year or check your phone three times a week?

**2335** WYR be "alone now" with Tiffany or be "the one and only" with Chesney Hawkes?

**2336** WYR be the President of the United States for a day or a billionaire for a day?

2337  WYR hold your horses or be like a bat out of hell?

2338  WYR look like a model but sound like Chewbacca or look like Chewbacca but sound like Donny and Marie?

2339  WYR have your face suddenly become pixelated or your voice suddenly become disguised on a first date?

2340  WYR watch lambs skipping in a meadow or fish jumping in a pond?

2341  WYR be an Englishman in New York or a New Yorker in London?

2342  WYR listen to the soundtrack from *Footloose* or *Guardians of the Galaxy*?

2343  WYR rather drink 7 UP or Mountain Dew?

2344  WYR be accused of being too optimistic or too pessimistic?

2345  WYR have a permanent itch on your nose or a permanently sweaty left foot?

2346  WYR be Zoom-bombed during an important video conference or be unable to turn off the cat-face filter?

2347  WYR only listen to sad songs or not listen to music at all?

2348  WYR be able to buy top-ups for emotions or buy upgrades for broken hearts?

2349  WYR have Iggy Pop's hair or Henry Rollins's tattoos?

2350  WYR eat the crust with the pizza or leave the crust until last?

2351  WYR use popular catchphrases from TV shows or create your own?

2352  WYR have barely legible handwriting but great typing skills or have beautiful handwriting and only be able to type with two fingers?

2353  WYR take a quick shower or a long bath?

2354  WYR always wear socks or never wear socks?

2355  WYR hop like a frog or hop on one leg?

2356  WYR have all your debt canceled or be free from all allergies?

**2357** WYR see a biographical movie of your favorite singer or read your favorite actor's autobiography?

**2358** WYR stick with your favorite brand or get paid to give your opinion on new brands?

**2359** WYR only own the few things you need or own lots of things even if you never use them?

**2360** WYR never lose anything again or never lose your temper?

**2361** WYR change your name for a different name or go by a nickname?

**2362** WYR be able to wiggle your ears or curl your tongue?

**2363** WYR be able to change the size of your feet or change the shape of your butt?

**2364** WYR go dancing for a night in the 1950s or the 1970s?

**2365** WYR be able to shrink your car to pocketsize when you're not driving or supersize yourself at will?

**2366** WYR be amazing at spelling or be able to do one amazing magic spell?

**2367** WYR buy expensive cologne or expensive face cream?

**2368** WYR do the job you do now or be able to snap your fingers and have the skills you need to change jobs?

**2369** WYR be the Last Jedi or the Last Boy Scout?

**2370** WYR trade places with a person or an animal?

**2371** WYR be able to ask your past self a single question or ask your future self a single question?

**2372** WYR visit the town of Nothing in Arizona or the town of Nowhere in Colorado?

**2373** WYR be obsessed with a hobby or obsessed with a TV show?

**2374** WYR be a talented liar or a talented lie detector?

**2375** WYR be a bookworm or go on a wormhole adventure?

**2376** WYR give up bread or give up all condiments?

2377  WYR stay as you are now or keep changing as you get older?

2378  WYR be known as the "picky eater" or the "glutton" in the family?

2379  WYR live in virtual reality where you are all-powerful or live in the real world and be able to go anywhere but not be able to interact with anyone or anything?

2380  WYR live in the town of Buttzville, New Jersey or Boogertown, North Carolina?

2381  WYR write a book or be the subject of a book?

2382  WYR look the same at forty as you did at twenty or look the same at eighty as you did at forty?

2383  WYR be a talented musical saw player or be able to crush apples in the crook of your elbow?

2384  WYR have someone tell you that you're smart or you're funny?

2385  WYR rather travel by motorboat or by yacht?

2386  WYR have eyebrows that can crawl around your face or hair that can fly away at random intervals?

2387  WYR be born with full-sized feet or full-sized ears that you have to grow into?

2388  WYR turn into a Lego figure for five minutes once a day or a cartoon character for one minute, five days a week?

2389  WYR have a fairy die or one of Santa's elves die every time you say you don't believe?

2390  WYR take a daily bath with a friendly hippo or go for a daily jog with a friendly emu?

2391  WYR have "Stayin' Alive" play at your funeral or "D-I-V-O-R-C-E" play at your wedding?

2392  WYR have your ears replaced with pork chops or your nose replaced with a meatball?

2393  WYR accidentally sit on fast-acting Gorilla Glue or wake up in the gorilla enclosure at the zoo?

2394  WYR unknowingly eat a ratburger or smell a rat in your kitchen?

**2395** WYR cry every time you laugh or fart every time you sneeze?

**2396** WYR be in the crow's nest on a ship in a sea storm or in an elevator when an earthquake strikes?

**2397** WYR ban fake tanning products or guyliner (eyeliner for men)?

**2398** WYR party like a boss or be The Boss (Bruce Springsteen)?

**2399** WYR look down your nose or put your foot in your mouth?

**2400** WYR travel by tractor or by tuk-tuk?

**2401** WYR eat food through your fingertips or breathe through your elbows?

**2402** WYR be "born to run" or "born to be wild"?

**2403** WYR listen to "sounds of the sixties" or "sounds of the seventies" on the radio?

**2404** WYR eat a lip balm sandwich or a Crayola sandwich?

**2405** WYR see feelings or feel sounds?

**2406** WYR only be able to watch re-runs of *Happy Days* or *Saved by the Bell* on TV?

**2407** WYR follow the instructions or throw caution to the wind?

**2408** WYR be a high diver who forgets how to swim or a racing driver who forgets how to drive?

**2409** WYR have Shrek's table manners or Sylvester the Cat's lisp?

**2410** WYR have the voice of an angel or make the best angel food cake?

**2411** WYR be able to give change for a dollar by putting it in your mouth or be able to breathe fire?

**2412** WYR have a bird in the hand or two in the bush?

**2413** WYR have an echo on everything you say or see double?

**2414** WYR be able to jive talk or moonwalk?

**2415** WYR stay at the Hotel California with The Eagles or Heartbreak Hotel with Elvis Presley?

2416 WYR have fingers that can snap and glow like glow sticks or hands that can spin around and sound like a soccer rattle?

2417 WYR have six fingers on your left hand or three fingers on your right hand?

2418 WYR give blood or take a trip down memory lane with a rambling aunt?

2419 WYR use mustard instead of hair gel or salad dressing instead of shower gel?

2420 WYR go on a voyage with Sinbad the Sailor or Jason and the Argonauts?

2421 WYR live in a world where nose-thumbing has replaced handshakes or the "whatever" forehead gesture has replaced "hello"?

2422 WYR live in a Dr. Seuss world or be Dr. Strange?

2423 WYR live the next ten years of your life in China or India?

2424 WYR only be able to watch badly dubbed kung fu movies or the original *King Kong* movie?

2425 WYR live in a world where there is no poverty and no TV or no hunger and no fast food?

2426 WYR it only ever rained at night or only ever snowed in January?

2427 WYR be able play guitar like Jimi Hendrix or write songs like Bob Dylan?

2428 WYR have the final say on who gets to star in movies or have control over who wins sporting championships?

2429 WYR eat to live or live to eat?

2430 WYR be unbeaten at Go Fish or Snap?

2431 WYR be the world's greatest sportsperson but explode after eating pizza or the world's greatest inventor but explode after eating cake?

2432 WYR be rockin', rollin', ridin' to Morningtown or rockin' all over the world?

**2433** WYR be a master at the art of origami or macramé?

**2434** WYR go bowling with Fred Flintstone or Uncle Buck?

**2435** WYR feel compelled to tango every time you hear a car horn or shout "Olé!" every time you cross a street?

**2436** WYR be caught telling a lie in the town of Embarrass, Minnesota or the town of Truth or Consequences in New Mexico?

**2437** WYR live in a different town in the state you're in now or live in a different state?

**2438** WYR inherit personality traits from your parents or your grandparents?

**2439** WYR have a permanent Snapchat filter on your face or have the "bloopers" of your daily life appear on YouTube?

**2440** WYR be "Lost in the Supermarket" or "Lost in Space"?

**2441** WYR have a magic compass that can lead you to anywhere you want to go or one that can lead you to whatever you want to find?

**2442** WYR be a one-eared rabbit or a one-eyed mouse?

**2443** WYR travel the world for a year with all expenses paid or have $500,000 to spend on whatever you want?

**2444** WYR step barefoot on a sea urchin or grab a thistle with bare hands?

**2445** WYR scale a poodle or a pangolin up to the size of a horse?

**2446** WYR have a perfect day or a perfect evening?

**2447** WYR be late for a meeting at work or late the first time you meet your partner's parents?

**2448** WYR have the world's biggest collection of sports memorabilia or army tanks?

**2449** WYR have the job of winding up the clocks in a clock museum or cleaning the mirrors in a hall of mirrors?

**2450** WYR break the world record for most CDs balanced on one finger or most socks put on one foot in one minute?

2451 WYR order pizza using Morse code or report to your boss using flag semaphore signals?

2452 WYR have hung out with Aretha Franklin and Ray Charles or Whitney Houston and Prince?

2453 WYR be in prison for a year or be in a coma for a year?

2454 WYR listen to all 154 of Shakespeare's sonnets or "Crazy Frog" on a loop?

2455 WYR live in a world without mashed potatoes or a world without pumpkin pie?

2456 WYR be the celebrity who starts the mass participation race or the celebrity who switches on the Christmas lights?

2457 WYR be like a fish out of water or be in hot water?

2458 WYR face your biggest fear for $1 million or do a picked-at-random dare for $2 million?

2459 WYR be able to change the color of glass by touching it or the temperature of a room by practicing singing scales?

2460 WYR listen to the tales of the *Arabian Nights* or *The Canterbury Tales*?

2461 WYR be able to control fire or water?

2462 WYR be able to dispense chocolate buttons from your belly button or blow Hershey's Kisses kisses?

2463 WYR trade places with Bart Simpson or Charlie Brown?

2464 WYR be a sight for sore eyes or catch someone's eye?

2465 WYR be known as the funky person in the group or the flaky person in the group?

2466 WYR be caught in an unexpected location or caught doing something surprising?

2467 WYR have a dream day of relaxation or have a day of action and adventure beyond your wildest dreams?

2468 WYR make one gargantuan decision right now or make one big decision every year with a coin toss?

**2469** WYR live in the Coen Brothers's version of *Fargo* or the remote town of Cicely in *Northern Exposure*?

**2470** WYR rehearse an important call before you make it or create an email draft to check before you send it?

**2471** WYR know the best place in town to have a picnic or the best place to drink cocktails?

**2472** WYR have Walt Disney's imagination or Jerry Seinfeld's wit?

**2473** WYR offer a friend career advice or personal advice?

**2474** WYR have your grandparents tell you the story of how they met or watch *How I Met Your Mother*?

**2475** WYR be living through the social isolation of 2020 or the social unrest of the 1960s?

**2476** WYR be able to meet a relative who died before you were born or be living the life you imagined when you were nine?

**2477** WYR be able to get your whole fist in your mouth or get your big toe in your mouth?

**2478** WYR have your mom teach you how to sew or learn from a YouTube tutorial?

**2479** WYR dance like Hugh Grant (David) in *Love Actually* or Tom Cruise (Joel) in *Risky Business*?

**2480** WYR name your pet fish Squishy or your pet dog Muttley?

**2481** WYR see the first artist you saw in concert again or the last artist you saw in concert?

**2482** WYR play two truths and a lie or charades?

**2483** WYR hide your embarrassment with a hand over your face or with a sweater pulled over your head?

**2484** WYR get into an argument with Angelica Pickles from *Rugrats* or Bubbles from *Powerpuff Girls*?

**2485** WYR have full control over what you'll watch on TV tonight or over what you'll have for dinner tonight?

2486 WYR wake up tomorrow having gained the ability to microwave meals with your eyes or jump like a cat?

2487 WYR be able to go back and change something your parents did or go back and change something you said to your parents?

2488 WYR have a magic eight ball that could answer questions for real or a crystal ball that could see your future for real?

2489 WYR get a tattoo of the pet you dreamed of having when you were five or of the person on your left?

2490 WYR cook your meals on a George Foreman grill or in an Instant Pot?

2491 WYR be able to erase a year in your life (unlive it) or erase three people (unmeet them)?

2492 WYR relive the best party you ever went to or the best family outing you ever went on?

2493 WYR own your favorite work of art or own something that once belonged to your favorite artist?

2494 WYR be tested on your spelling ability right now or your math ability right now?

2495 WYR be able to buy one object, no matter the price, or meet one person (dead or alive)?

2496 WYR fend off a grumpy baboon or a grumpy badger?

2497 WYR be able to choose the gender of your unborn baby or their physical features?

2498 WYR have a bathroom big enough to play baseball in or a private jet with a bedroom in it?

2499 WYR hold the record for the fastest time to place twenty-four cans in a fridge or fastest time to drink two pints of water?

2500 WYR hang out with John-Boy Walton or Billy Ray Cyrus?

2501 WYR be Mighty Mouse or Woody Woodpecker?

2502 WYR have written a play or had an article published in a magazine?

2503 WYR be able to read and write Latin or breakdance?

**2504** WYR have achieved a perfect score in a math test or won an eating contest?

**2505** WYR be a professionally trained actor having to appear in a commercial or having to be the voiceover in a commercial?

**2506** WYR take ballet lessons to become more graceful or take up rowing to improve your stamina?

**2507** WYR not be able to swim or not be able to ride a bicycle?

**2508** WYR be able to hold your breath for two minutes or run a mile in under seven minutes?

**2509** WYR be able to cartwheel with ease or juggle with six knives?

**2510** WYR live in a theater or a watermill?

**2511** WYR be voted most likely to succeed in high school or hold the record for the most saltine crackers eaten in one minute?

**2512** WYR only watch black-and-white movies or only own black cars?

**2513** WYR never visit New York City or never go on a rollercoaster?

**2514** WYR have a house full of house plants or a house full of cats?

**2515** WYR go out in a cape-and-cane ensemble or wearing tights instead of pants?

**2516** WYR only eat raw potato or only ever eat cooked (never raw) tomatoes?

**2517** WYR not have a Netflix account or never leave dirty dishes in the sink?

**2518** WYR never win a contest of any kind or never get a ticket of any kind?

**2519** WYR only cook once each week or only cook with a deep fryer?

**2520** WYR drizzle honey or sprinkle cilantro on all food?

**2521** WYR have written two books or climbed four mountains?

**2522** WYR have a pet peacock or visit Bangkok?

**2523** WYR pay with the exact change or never have anything smaller than a $20 bill?

**2524** WYR not be able to whistle or not be able to snap your fingers?

**2525** WYR meet Tom Cruise or go on a river cruise?

**2526** WYR be famous when you are alive and forgotten when you die or unknown when you are alive but famous after you die?

**2527** WYR be tired no matter how much you sleep or constantly hungry no matter how much you eat?

**2528** WYR never use a public restroom or never give a speech in public?

**2529** WYR spread the rumor that one of your relations is a secret agent or Keanu Reeves?

**2530** WYR take part in a murder mystery weekend or ride in the Mystery Machine with Scooby-Doo?

**2531** WYR visit Disneyland on your own or eat out at a restaurant on your own?

**2532** WYR spend fifteen minutes trying to catch a fly or spend fifteen minutes on hold on the phone?

**2533** WYR play the harmonica or sing acapella?

**2534** WYR take part in a mud wrestling contest or make a Mississippi mud pie?

**2535** WYR have tea with Julia Roberts or coffee with George Clooney?

**2536** WYR go ice fishing or learn how to make ice sculptures?

**2537** WYR be able to name every U.S state capital or hold the record for the fastest time to type the alphabet backwards on an iPad?

**2538** WYR always go to bed before 10 pm or always eat chocolate chip pancakes for breakfast?

**2539** WYR spend two years with your soulmate before they die, leaving you to never love again, or spend your life with someone nice you settled for?

**2540** WYR own a convertible or a monster truck?

**2541** WYR hold the record for the most times jumped into a pair of underwear in thirty seconds or the most tennis balls held in one hand?

**2542** WYR never break a bone or never break a promise?

**2543** WYR eat oysters or own a natural pearl?

**2544** WYR be able to play a guitar with your teeth or behind your back?

**2545** WYR be able to touch your nose with your tongue or play the flute with your nose?

**2546** WYR have a fear of anything that jumps or anything that beeps?

**2547** WYR hold the record for the fastest time to assemble Mr. Potato Head while blindfolded or play Blindman's Buff?

**2548** WYR browse inside a china shop with Calamity Jane or Mr. Bean?

**2549** WYR never get divorced or never meet your soulmate?

**2550** WYR your spirit animal was an inchworm or a dung beetle?

**2551** WYR eat an entire watermelon in one sitting or put hot sauce on everything you eat for a week?

**2552** WYR be able to impersonate every *Simpsons* character or every *South Park* character?

**2553** WYR be able to teach an old dog new tricks or be an expert at the "walk the dog" yo-yo trick?

**2554** WYR dance a polka every day at noon for a week or wear only polka dot clothing for a week?

**2555** WYR eat the world's stinkiest cheese or down a whole jar of pickles in one sitting?

**2556** WYR have a cat named Tabby McTat or a dog named Scruff McGruff?

**2557** WYR be a member of the fashion police or the grammar police?

**2558** WYR know how to fix cars or how to outfox the opposition?

**2559** WYR be able to get twenty-four marshmallows in your mouth at once or stack forty-four dice using chopsticks?

**2560** WYR never be too old to laugh when ketchup makes a fart sound or be old enough to know better?

**2561** WYR never have major surgery or never go into a Walmart ever again?

**2562** WYR have a TV in every room in your house or have a room in your house just for shoes?

**2563** WYR stick by the golden rule or have a golden goose?

**2564** WYR be able to reverse one decision every day or be able to pause time for a minute every day?

**2565** WYR spend a day at a roller rink or a drive-in movie theater?

**2566** WYR bungee jump from a hot air balloon or make balloon animals?

**2567** WYR eat a side of mushrooms with every meal or have anchovies on every meal?

**2568** WYR have a blast or get a blast from the past?

**2569** WYR have a fear of buttons or feel compelled to push all buttons (especially big red ones)?

**2570** WYR carry the Olympic torch or be the Human Torch?

**2571** WYR eat a spoonful of wasabi or a spoonful of Tabasco sauce?

**2572** WYR be the life and soul of the party but secretly feel depressed or have people think you're boring while you're really content with life?

**2573** WYR live in a house with creaky floorboards or a house with bifold glass doors?

**2574** WYR only be able to read romance novels or be the author of romance novels?

**2575** WYR walk backwards up steps or go down steps two at a time?

**2576** WYR play the piano standing up or with your eyes closed?

**2577** WYR be "dancing in the dark" or "dancing in the street"?

**2578** WYR make Hulk Hogan or David Bannerman angry?

**2579** WYR not have a middle name or have six middle names?

**2580** WYR have your ducks in a row or duck and dive?

**2581** WYR be a driving instructor or a diving instructor?

**2582** WYR be addicted to eating dirt or eating soap?

**2583** WYR live on Sesame Street or in Bikini Bottom?

**2584** WYR be a straight-A student or a member of the A-Team?

**2585** WYR have a fear of water or be addicted to eating ice?

**2586** WYR bowl a strike or serve a tennis ace?

**2587** WYR be a catwalk model or make model cats?

**2588** WYR always use the rule of thumb or have a green thumb?

**2589** WYR be a fish that could wish or a pig that could fly?

**2590** WYR make it law that children should be seen and not heard or people over the age of seventy-five shouldn't drive?

**2591** WYR be a jump rope champion or a horse jumping champion?

**2592** WYR be taller than your parents or have your children be taller than you?

**2593** WYR be under someone's thumb or stand out like a sore thumb?

**2594** WYR play by the rules or bend the rules?

**2595** WYR be dressed to the nines or go the whole nine yards?

**2596** WYR be the underdog or a dark horse?

**2597** WYR not know how to cook or not know how to drive?

**2598** WYR lose all your teeth or all your hair?

**2599** WYR have read 300 books or have bowled a perfect 300 game?

**2600** WYR be a cheerleader with a sore throat or a sound technician with a sore ear?

**2601** WYR not wear deodorant or not wear underwear?

**2602** WYR be in a high school anime club or an improv club?

**2603** WYR be only able to whisper or only able to shout?

**2604** WYR never gain weight or never get sick?

**2605** WYR collect rocks or rock 'n' roll memorabilia?

**2606** WYR prepare a Thanksgiving meal for twelve people or give a speech in front of 112 people?

**2607** WYR be able to do a back handspring or go back in time by five minutes by clapping your hands?

**2608** WYR spend an hour people watching or cloud watching?

**2609** WYR be able to catch fish in your mouth like a bear or catch fish with your talons like an osprey?

**2610** WYR have invented Band-Aids or Kool-Aid?

**2611** WYR have to say the alphabet backwards without hesitation or list all fifty U.S. states alphabetically?

**2612** WYR own thirty pairs of socks or thirty hats?

**2613** WYR make the best mac and cheese in the world or the best key lime pie?

**2614** WYR have been the first passenger to ride on a train or the first person to use an escalator?

**2615** WYR eat a well-done steak if you prefer it rare or eggs over easy if you prefer them sunny side up?

**2616** WYR eat red chili peppers or listen to the Red Hot Chili Peppers?

**2617** WYR be able to swim like the Man from Atlantis or run like The Six Million Dollar Man?

**2618** WYR cut your own hair or valet your boss's car?

**2619** WYR ride the world's tallest roller coaster or a mechanical bull on its toughest setting?

**2620** WYR be a fairy living in a toadstool house or a witch living in a gingerbread house?

**2621**  WYR find your dream job or true love?

**2622**  WYR drink a pot of coffee at breakfast or eat a stack of six pancakes every morning?

**2623**  WYR be ten years older than your sibling or ten years younger?

**2624**  WYR be someone's rock or rock the boat?

**2625**  WYR be a stand-up comedian or a one-man band?

**2626**  WYR be a "beauty school dropout" or a homecoming queen?

**2627**  WYR paddle with ducks or swim with swans?

**2628**  WYR be a wannabe ventriloquist or a wannabe contortionist?

**2629**  WYR never own a house or never own a car?

**2630**  WYR kiss a crocodile or tickle a bear?

**2631**  WYR have three cars or be one of the Three Amigos?

**2632**  WYR be a cheesemaker or a winemaker?

**2633**  WYR watch *The Sound of Music* or *The Great Escape*?

**2634**  WYR be an art freak or be a freakshow on the dance floor?

**2635**  WYR have a bad haircut or wear ugly shoes?

**2636**  WYR meet John Travolta as Danny in *Grease* or Tony in *Saturday Night Fever*?

**2637**  WYR eat dim sum or teriyaki chicken?

**2638**  WYR ride in a motorcycle sidecar or on an elephant?

**2639**  WYR have a bubblegum pop hit or an indie pop hit?

**2640**  WYR spend money on a vacation or a new TV?

**2641**  WYR eat baked Alaska or baked chocolate bread in Alaska?

**2642**  WYR store cups right side up or upside down?

**2643**  WYR have a disco glitter ball or an illuminated disco dance floor?

**2644** WYR be a competitor with a serious game face or a spectator posting images of your game face on Instagram?

**2645** WYR have muscular legs and weak arms or muscular arms and weak legs?

**2646** WYR be bow-legged or knock-kneed?

**2647** WYR be a city slicker or a country bumpkin?

**2648** WYR be the hider or the seeker in a game of hide and seek?

**2649** WYR have freshly cut flowers on display or have artificial flower displays?

**2650** WYR rename Facebook or rename TikTok?

**2651** WYR walk the talk or walk the line?

**2652** WYR listen to classical music or visit a modern art gallery?

**2653** WYR spend a whole day at the mall or a whole day in the kitchen cooking up a storm?

**2654** WYR share a loveseat with a smelly cat or a bed with a gassy dog?

**2655** WYR go for a beer (soda) with your favorite football player or favorite basketball player?

**2656** WYR eat trail mix or pick 'n' mix (penny candy)?

**2657** WYR snail mail became obsolete or money became obsolete (card payments only)?

**2658** WYR driverless cars for all or real-time translator apps for all came first?

**2659** WYR rock out to rap or rap to rock?

**2660** WYR have been part of *The Brady Bunch* or the *Hair Bear Bunch*?

**2661** WYR be shy or work-shy?

**2662** WYR read the book or watch the movie?

**2663** WYR never marry or never have children?

**2664** WYR your pet lived twice as long as normal or was twice as intelligent as normal?

**2665** WYR have your pride hurt or have to swallow your pride?

**2666** WYR never remember someone's face or always forget their name?

**2667** WYR only ever have vanilla ice cream or strawberry ice cream?

**2668** WYR tie a sweater around your waist or a scarf around your neck?

**2669** WYR be sitting on a gold mine or be worth your weight in gold?

**2670** WYR see blue roses or red violets?

**2671** WYR have noodles with Kung Fu Panda or pizza with Michelangelo the Teenage Mutant Ninja Turtle?

**2672** WYR eat French toast or German sausage?

**2673** WYR be weird and wacky or shrewd and sagacious?

**2674** WYR eat surf and turf or surf the waves?

**2675** WYR ban flower farming or almond farming?

**2676** WYR stop doing something you do daily or start doing something new on top of what you do daily?

**2677** WYR save the day Mighty Mouse-style or Underdog-style?

**2678** WYR have to run to save your life or eat food out of a trash can to survive?

**2679** WYR daydream about things you've done or things you'd like to do?

**2680** WYR clean rest stop toilets or a slaughterhouse for a living?

**2681** WYR have an Xbox or a PlayStation if you could have only one?

**2682** WYR spent the night in Hotel Transylvania or The Best Exotic Marigold Hotel?

**2683** WYR visit the land of the rising sun or the land of milk and honey?

**2684** WYR be able to grow at will or be able to shrink at will?

2685  WYR hear the sound of silence or the sound of children playing?

2686  WYR have no eyebrows or no eyelashes?

2687  WYR snicker like Muttley or giggle like Elmo?

2688  WYR eat fruit salad or potato salad?

2689  WYR be able to see what is behind every door or be able to open all doors by saying "Open sesame!"?

2690  WYR not use your smartphone for a week or be stung by a jellyfish?

2691  WYR never use another emoji or never laugh again?

2692  WYR win a trip to Hawaii or win the latest Huawei phone?

2693  WYR be a school janitor or a kennel maid?

2694  WYR have a job that pays $100 an hour but lets you work from home or a job that pays $180 an hour but requires you to be physically present?

2695  WYR set your hair on fire or crack your phone screen?

2696  WYR throw up on an airplane or get kicked by a horse?

2697  WYR walk for two hours or sit in traffic for two hours?

2698  WYR be as good as gold or be born with a silver spoon in your mouth?

2699  WYR accidently injure yourself trying to impress someone or trying to text and walk?

2700  WYR find a crocodile in your swimming pool or a snake in your car?

2701  WYR have hair long enough to sit on or an antique chaise longue stuffed with horsehair?

2702  WYR get to help Santa deliver presents or get to help the Easter bunny hide chocolate eggs?

2703  WYR have the antagonist in your novel be known to dine and dash or shoplift?

2704  WYR be a wise owl or a playful puppy?

**2705** WYR have the odds stacked against you or be the odd one out?

**2706** WYR get lost in the pages of a book for four hours or lose four hours on Facebook?

**2707** WYR never steal a robe from a hotel or never steal a kiss from someone who is in a relationship?

**2708** WYR visit a country in Africa or Asia?

**2709** WYR save someone from drowning or save a goal in soccer so your team wins?

**2710** WYR look through Alice's looking glass or look after 101 Dalmatians?

**2711** WYR ban bubblegum pop music or ban popcorn in movie theaters?

**2712** WYR create a "common courtesy award" for people who hold doors open for others or drivers who let others into a line of traffic?

**2713** WYR be an urban fox or Keith Urban's guitar?

**2714** WYR have writer's block or be one of Ian Dury's Blockheads?

**2715** WYR be stranded in a desert with just a pocketknife or stranded in a jungle with only a rope?

**2716** WYR discover the universe was a giant board game or a computer simulation?

**2717** WYR be trapped in an underwater cave with only thirty seconds of air or three hours of air and no hope of rescue?

**2718** WYR come face to face with a shark or a silverback gorilla?

**2719** WYR try to escape from the Temple of Doom with Indiana Jones or escape from the KGB with James Bond?

**2720** WYR live in Whoville (Dr. Seuss) or Thneedville?

**2721** WYR run along a beach to the original *Baywatch* theme or drive through Beverly Hills to the *Beverly Hills, 90210* theme?

**2722** WYR be skilled in the use of a boomerang or own a retro 1980s boombox?

**2723** WYR have a smoke alarm that makes the sound of Fred Flintstone yelling "Yabba dabba doo!" or Dave yelling "Alvin!"?

**2724** WYR a cloud of flies descended upon you whenever you said "and" or a swarm of crickets whenever you said "but"?

**2725** WYR be Boo-Boo Bear or Thumper the rabbit?

**2726** WYR have Jimmy Osmond as your "Long Haired Lover from Liverpool" or travel with Shirley Temple "On the Good Ship Lollipop"?

**2727** WYR be the only person in town who doesn't have a car or the only person in town who does have a car?

**2728** WYR fly on the back of a Great Eagle or fly off the end of a ski jump like Eddie the Eagle?

**2729** WYR have Mary Poppins's magic carpet bag or flying umbrella?

**2730** WYR only have hotel-sized shampoo bottles or watermelon-sized onions?

**2731** WYR count your steps out loud as you walk or count backwards from ten before going through any door?

**2732** WYR be able to travel through time or through dimensions?

**2733** WYR be assimilated by the Borg or attacked by the Death Star?

**2734** WYR be frugal or stubborn?

**2735** WYR never smile for pictures or never find money down the back of the couch?

**2736** WYR chew the end of your pen or pen your thoughts?

**2737** WYR be able to change the oil in your car or change a photo into an oil painting?

**2738** WYR do Pilates or eat pierogi (Polish dumplings)?

**2739** WYR be a bathrobe or a pair of slippers?

**2740** WYR eat sunflower seeds or grow a sunflower?

**2741** WYR peanuts tasted like garden peas or corn dogs tasted like sweet corn?

**2742** WYR smell the aroma of burning incense or hear the sound of wind chimes?

**2743** WYR make snickerdoodles or watch Snagglepuss?

**2744** WYR snack on Gorgonzola or ride in a gondola?

**2745** WYR push a button and be magically transported up any stairs or pull a lever and be magically transported across town?

**2746** WYR have Nyan Cat or Pusheen as a pet?

**2747** WYR always get away with lying or always get tickets for the shows you want to see?

**2748** WYR snack on green olives or green peppers?

**2749** WYR live in an Amish community for a week or a Buddhist retreat for a week?

**2750** WYR follow a will-o'-the-wisp or stay on the beaten path?

**2751** WYR your hair never tangled or your feet never got cheesy?

**2752** WYR be a guinea pig that could fly or a chipmunk that could sing?

**2753** WYR work twelve-hour shifts for three days each week or work offshore for three weeks and have three weeks off?

**2754** WYR go line dancing with Shania Twain or belly dancing with Shakira?

**2755** WYR be an old lady's cat or the Hello Kitty cat?

**2756** WYR see imaginary spiders or feel imaginary spiders?

**2757** WYR play chicken or have chickenpox?

**2758** WYR scream out loud in a movie theater or ugly cry in a movie theater?

**2759** WYR your parents never cried happy tears or your children never cried sad tears?

**2760** WYR never fire a gun or never be mugged?

**2761** WYR create a punishment for people who take all the red Skittles or people who leave an empty toilet roll holder?

2762 WYR wear a party hat to work (school) or Crocs to a party?

2763 WYR have a huge imagination or a photographic memory?

2764 WYR pay twice as much for plane tickets or never fly again?

2765 WYR have a full body wax or wax five cars by hand?

2766 WYR push over someone's snowman or step on someone's sandcastle?

2767 WYR get rid of one bad habit or gain one new good habit?

2768 WYR have actual butterfingers or actual fish fingers?

2769 WYR sleep on a pillow stuffed with kitty litter or sawdust?

2770 WYR play music on shuffle or do the Harlem Shuffle?

2771 WYR be a scarf in a lost property box or in a thrift store?

2772 WYR hike the entire Appalachian Trail or watch all one hundred episodes of *The Roy Rogers Show*?

2773 WYR have 330 people at your family reunion or thirty-three?

2774 WYR study beetles or play Beetle (Cootie)?

2775 WYR it rained lost socks or socks could wash themselves?

2776 WYR sleepwalk or sleep talk?

2777 WYR date someone with the same name as one of your siblings or the same name as your dog?

2778 WYR live in a world where sheep work in barbershops or horses work in car sales?

2779 WYR communicate your hobbies through Pictionary or Creationary (Lego)?

2780 WYR be named after a color or a virtue?

2781 WYR earn someone's respect or earn someone's gratitude?

2782 WYR end all illegal animal trading or have your favorite animal become extinct?

2783  WYR binge-watch TV all day or binge on junk food all day?

2784  WYR jam with Bob Marley or the Grateful Dead?

2785  WYR have a strong opinion or sit on the fence?

2786  WYR be all at sea or between the devil and the deep blue sea?

2787  WYR ban the word "bossy" or the phrase "blue sky thinking"?

2788  WYR have spaghetti without sauce or a bun without a burger?

2789  WYR ban the phrase "at the end of the day" or the word "totally"?

2790  WYR knock over the first domino in someone's long line or knock down someone's house of cards?

2791  WYR be a migrating wildebeest or a migrating goose?

2792  WYR dance the fandango or sing the *Fraggle Rock* opening theme?

2793  WYR not be able to use a corkscrew or a can opener?

2794  WYR never have another bad thought or never get invited to another good party?

2795  WYR be considered "gifted" or "special"?

2796  WYR be hypercritical or a hypocrite?

2797  WYR be a spring flower or a fall leaf?

2798  WYR have a chessboard or a Clue board with life-size playing pieces?

2799  WYR be half-human, half-fly or a reverse mermaid (merman)?

2800  WYR be someone to rely on or be reliably unreliable?

2801  WYR drink Scotch on the rocks with "The Rock" or drink martinis with Martin Scorsese?

2802  WYR never bite off more than you can chew or never bite the hand that feeds?

2803  WYR face the Spanish Inquisition or "The Wrath of Khan"?

**2804** WYR be Rubik of Rubik's Cube or Graham of Graham crackers?

**2805** WYR not be able to open any closed doors or not be able to close any open doors?

**2806** WYR compromise on where you live or where you go on vacation?

**2807** WYR give up on a personal goal or sacrifice a work goal to achieve a personal goal?

**2808** WYR dress as a Viking or as a Marvel character for a day?

**2809** WYR have an actual sheepdog (sheep mixed with dog) or an actual bird dog (bird mixed with dog)?

**2810** WYR see a bunny that can jive or a chicken that can dance?

**2811** WYR be true to your zodiac sign or your Chinese zodiac animal?

**2812** WYR be an expert calligrapher or an expert bingo caller?

**2813** WYR dance the hoochie coochie or drink hooch?

**2814** WYR dance like Pee-wee Herman or sing like Angelica Pickles?

**2815** WYR hold a grudge or hold the record for "the most sticky notes on the face in one minute"?

**2816** WYR be a soccer goalie or an ice hockey goalie?

**2817** WYR be someone who gets the ball rolling or someone who can roll with the punches?

**2818** WYR be impressive or be an impressionist?

**2819** WYR help Mystery, Inc. solve a mystery or The Goonies?

**2820** WYR have your face slammed into a cake or have a door slammed in your face?

**2821** WYR put your finger into a yawning dog's mouth or kiss a duck?

**2822** WYR ride on the roof of a car or ride in a supermarket shopping cart?

**2823** WYR eat food in a supermarket before paying for it or crash a wedding party?

**2824** WYR pee outdoors or pee in the sink?

**2825** WYR wear socks with toes or barefoot running shoes?

**2826** WYR dress up as a robber with a stocking on your head or as a bandit with a dish towel as a poncho?

**2827** WYR eat a brilliant meal in a bad restaurant or an awful meal in an amazing restaurant?

**2828** WYR dress in a single color or always wear a hat?

**2829** WYR put something on the stove and forget about it or fall asleep in the sun and get burned?

**2830** WYR see a hedgehog drinking milk or see a swimming pig?

**2831** WYR get your tongue pierced or be a nude life model in an art class?

**2832** WYR see a baby being born or a cactus bloom?

**2833** WYR not be able to tie a tie or not be able to tie shoelaces?

**2834** WYR drive a limousine or drive a hard bargain?

**2835** WYR be seated next to a dog or a chicken on a plane?

**2836** WYR visit a shadow theater or play *Pokémon Go*?

**2837** WYR eat shark meat or eat mustard on its own?

**2838** WYR be Jerry from *Tom and Jerry* or Benny the Ball from *Top Cat*?

**2839** WYR have extrasensory abilities or be able to jump rope effortlessly for fifteen minutes?

**2840** WYR dry a wet dog with a blow dryer or rescue a kitten from a tall tree?

**2841** WYR wear Prada or drive a Ferrari?

**2842** WYR be able to do a breakdance suicide drop or drop the mic at the end of a speech?

**2843** WYR play the "floor is lava" game or the "don't let the balloon touch the floor" game?

**2844** WYR go night diving with a buddy or meet a date on a skyscraper roof?

**2845** WYR watch the Discovery Channel or spend a night on a beach?

**2846** WYR dress pets in designer outfits or work in a veterinary clinic?

**2847** WYR kiss in the back row at a movie theater or kiss under the mistletoe on Christmas Eve?

**2848** WYR have a song played for you on the radio or write a song that gets played on the radio?

**2849** WYR iron your shoelaces or organize your kitchen cupboard contents alphabetically?

**2850** WYR have a partner who snores in bed or talks in their sleep?

**2851** WYR be "The Music Man" or know "The Muffin Man"?

**2852** WYR celebrate your weekday birthday on the day or have a party on the weekend?

**2853** WYR be a fast talker or a slow eater?

**2854** WYR live in a shell for life like a snail or shift from shell to shell through life like a hermit crab?

**2855** WYR be a hammerhead shark or a bottlenose dolphin?

**2856** WYR see the sites on vacation or taste the local delicacies?

**2857** WYR let it go or fight tooth and nail to hold on to it?

**2858** WYR know the true meaning of freedom or the true meaning of peace?

**2859** WYR give up your most prized possession or give up a $100,000 prize?

**2860** WYR never doubt yourself or never do anything spontaneous?

**2861** WYR enjoy simple pleasures or strive to experience the finer things in life?

**2862** WYR be your own worst enemy or have a lifelong arch nemesis?

**2863** WYR have a heart of glass or look at the world through rose-tinted glasses?

**2864** WYR never tell a white lie or never see red?

**2865** WYR have someone to watch over you or watch the world go by with friends?

**2866** WYR hit the dance floor or hit the hay?

**2867** WYR accidentally break a window or spill ketchup on your friend's white top?

**2868** WYR share food with your dog or share your bed with a cat?

**2869** WYR be able to talk your way out of trouble or be a guest on a talk show?

**2870** WYR be someone who can't hit the broad side of a barn or someone who is prone to hitting the roof?

**2871** WYR have an attic full of things to remind you of your past or just one photograph?

**2872** WYR grow old gracefully or be the oldest swinger in town?

**2873** WYR fall on hard times or fall from grace?

**2874** WYR lie about your likes and dislikes on a date or lie about your experience in a job interview?

**2875** WYR learn how to play a different sport or learn how to do a new dance?

**2876** WYR become a politician or a police officer?

**2877** WYR wipe a social network off the face of the earth or wipe the floor with someone?

**2878** WYR never be depressed or never have to eat humble pie?

**2879** WYR play hardball or play hard to get?

**2880** WYR have a secret garden or visit the Garden of the Gods Nature Center in Colorado?

**2881** WYR post pictures of everything you eat on social media or look at other people's vacation pictures?

2882 WYR kiss and tell or kiss something goodbye?

2883 WYR not care what you wear or not care about what others think of you?

2884 WYR have culinary skills or skateboard skills?

2885 WYR play Clue with Sherlock Holmes or Twister with Stretch Armstrong?

2886 WYR never have to steal or never have to beg?

2887 WYR bring back James Dean or James Brown?

2888 WYR be a couch potato or a backseat driver?

2889 WYR ban Disney singers or people who speak in clichés?

2890 WYR hear the details of a real-life scandal or watch a scandal unfold in a TV drama?

2891 WYR be given funding to pay for a study course or be given vouchers for a lifetime supply of pizza?

2892 WYR be a snitcher or a brown-noser?

2893 WYR have to give store cashiers a gift whenever you make a purchase or give all hitchhikers a ride?

2894 WYR live in a world where bananas have replaced money or where kittens and puppies never grow into cats and dogs?

2895 WYR applaud the sunrise every morning or write a thank-you note to the kettle whenever it boils?

2896 WYR feel compelled to pet bald people on the head or ruffle the hair of everyone wearing a suit?

2897 WYR have gummy bears for teeth or have no teeth?

2898 WYR show ID to a bouncer to enter your home or have an aggressive dog waiting outside your home?

2899 WYR wear a seventeenth-century wig to work or wear a string of raw tiger prawns around your neck?

2900 WYR only be able to eat while you are running or only after completing a 500-piece jigsaw?

**2901** WYR take an exam based on user manual contents before using a new device or have a brick-sized smartphone?

**2902** WYR eat a mouthful of dust from your vacuum cleaner bag once a week or eat using a dustpan and brush?

**2903** WYR only flush your toilet once a day or walk around everywhere carrying a toilet roll under your arm?

**2904** WYR sleep in a Dracula-style coffin or pee the bed once a week?

**2905** WYR drag an anchor behind you everywhere you go or wave at everyone you see?

**2906** WYR eat ten Kit Kat bars or go to a bar run by ten cats?

**2907** WYR only be able to read odd-numbered pages or only be able to buy items from the bottom shelf in stores?

**2908** WYR your canine teeth tripled in size or you had to wear a dog recovery cone for a week?

**2909** WYR only be able to eat cold food for the rest of your life or only able to take cold showers?

**2910** WYR only be able to see in the dark or only be able to buy one item each time you go to the supermarket?

**2911** WYR have sand in your underpants or honey in your footwear?

**2912** WYR have eyes bigger than your belly or be under a spotlight wherever you go?

**2913** WYR never be able to set foot on dry land again or feel seasick whenever you take a shower?

**2914** WYR only be able to speak a hundred words a day or have to count a thousand sheep before you can get to sleep?

**2915** WYR feel compelled to pick your nose when talking or compelled to lick someone's hand after shaking it?

**2916** WYR lick all your plates clean or always have a soapy taste in your mouth?

**2917** WYR only be able to dress in knitted nettles or wear a sheepskin rug?

2918　WYR spray toilet freshener on yourself every day or have a bird poop on you every day?

2919　WYR deliberately trip up a stranger every day or have to talk nonstop all day?

2920　WYR bark at people entering your home or pee with excitement when people enter your home?

2921　WYR have everything you drop be gone forever or be unable to say goodbye to your workmates every day without crying?

2922　WYR be unable to separate your fingers or have your feet stick to the floor after thirty seconds of non-movement?

2923　WYR have your eyes stay closed for five seconds whenever you blink or your mouth stay open for five minutes when you yawn?

2924　WYR get a permanent Santa Claus tattoo on your shoulder or sprout a Salvador Dali-style mustache?

2925　WYR burst into tears or burst into song whenever you're hungry?

2926　WYR fart the sound of a foghorn or have your home permanently surrounded by fog?

2927　WYR hear a buzzer every time something touches your lips or make a beeping sound when you chew?

2928　WYR feel compelled to play dead whenever you hear a siren or feel compelled to steal candy from children whenever you hear a siren?

2929　WYR be trapped in a room full of spiders or one filled with snakes?

2930　WYR be unable to make any facial expressions or start drooling whenever you see someone you like?

2931　WYR everything you ate tasted like potato or everything you ate had to be blended?

2932　WYR have your shoelaces tied together or wear a watermelon helmet?

2933　WYR have onion and pickles on everything you eat or find a grub hiding in everything you eat?

2934　WYR find bones in your fish or cat hairs in your coffee?

**2935** WYR babies cry when you look at them or dogs howl when you go near them?

**2936** WYR go upstairs on your hands and knees or go downstairs on your butt?

**2937** WYR chug everything you drink or have your mouth stay open all day?

**2938** WYR unlock your phone by singing "Humpty Dumpty" or by typing in the code using your toes?

**2939** WYR have only strobe lights in your home or only be able to listen to music at full volume?

**2940** WYR have six mosquitos in your bedroom every night or have your clothes always feel itchy?

**2941** WYR create a punishment for people who jump lines or people who shout into their phones?

**2942** WYR have a dollar added to your bank account every time you fart or be given $1 back for every $10 you spend?

**2943** WYR hold someone's hand for a full three minutes when shaking hands or hold your breath for thirty seconds?

**2944** WYR feel compelled to chase every pigeon you see or bark at every dog?

**2945** WYR eat breakfast in the shower or brush your teeth in bed?

**2946** WYR socks came out of the laundry already sorted into pairs or toilets self-cleaned?

**2947** WYR receive a complimentary drink or a complimentary slice of bologna whenever you enter a building?

**2948** WYR go through airport security with no clothes on or only eat airplane food on vacation?

**2949** WYR wake up with an upside-down face or with your arms and legs attached backwards?

**2950** WYR go to work on a hippity-hop or by jumping in a sack?

**2951** WYR have a mariachi band or a solo trombonist follow you around?

**2952** WYR use pancake syrup or raw egg in place of face cream?

**2953** WYR prance like a pony when you cross the street or hop like a penguin when you go down steps?

**2954** WYR have the feeling you're being watched by a horse on a hill or be afraid to go to the bathroom on your own?

**2955** WYR make the sound of jingling bells when you move or "Ho! Ho! Ho!" when you laugh on the run-up to Christmas?

**2956** WYR get an electric shock every time you receive a text message or every time you touch someone?

**2957** WYR spend a day with everything in life moving in slow motion or a day when you do everything twice as fast?

**2958** WYR have your eyebrows replaced with bread crusts or always smell slightly of ferret?

**2959** WYR get a one-off one minute of free shopping in a store of your choice or a personal assistant for a week?

**2960** WYR feel compelled to yell "Shark!" whenever you swim in the sea or "Stick 'em up!" whenever you go into a bank?

**2961** WYR have a neighbor who's learning to play the drums or the bagpipes?

**2962** WYR call an ambulance whenever you break a nail or the police whenever you lose a sock?

**2963** WYR it rained indoors as well as outdoors or you hiccupped constantly every time it rained?

**2964** WYR store your meals in your cheeks like a hamster or run on a hamster wheel to power your home?

**2965** WYR lose your internet connection whenever you open the fridge door or have the fuses blow every time you sneeze?

**2966** WYR chew on bamboo all day like a panda or carry a life-size stuffed panda with you all day?

**2967** WYR make a balloon animal for every toddler you meet or do a magic trick for every teenager you meet?

**2968** WYR say your pin number out loud whenever you pay by card or listen to the cashier's personal problems?

**2969** WYR develop an irrational fear of trash cans or be afraid of your own shadow?

**2970** WYR have the music stop whenever you get up to dance or have a fly go in your mouth every time you yawn?

**2971** WYR carry a rose between your teeth or burp loudly whenever you speak?

**2972** WYR sit on someone's lap on public transport or have your feet overheat if you stand still for over five minutes?

**2973** WYR be able to remember everything in every book you read or remember every conversation you have?

**2974** WYR eat food you pick up off the street or sleep on a bed of rocks?

**2975** WYR live in a garden shed or a greenhouse?

**2976** WYR wake up every morning with a new $100 bill in your pocket but not know where it came from or wake up every morning with a new $50 bill in your pocket and know where it came from?

**2977** WYR everyone always laughed at your jokes or you received at least once compliment every day?

**2978** WYR decorate your head like an Easter egg at Easter or sing "Holidays are coming . . ." every time you drink a Coke?

**2979** WYR every towel you use be damp or all paint you touch be wet?

**2980** WYR be able to take pictures by blinking your eyes or memorize words by running your finger over them?

**2981** WYR not be able to use (speak or write) the letter "w" or have everything you say repeated back to you?

**2982** WYR have a small snail living in your ear or a small worm living in your nose?

**2983** WYR not shower for a week or not brush your teeth for a week?

**2984** WYR wake up with a rooster's comb on your head or with all of your body fat gathered under your chin?

**2985** WYR start speaking in street slang during every conversation or have your computer turn off automatically every time you misspell a word?

**2986** WYR take one step back after every two steps forward or clap your hands in time with every step you take?

**2987** WYR only be able to wear leather or only be able to talk when you're breathing in?

**2988** WYR be woken up every morning by a drooling dog or pet sit twenty guinea pigs for a month?

**2989** WYR have to pick up all the trash you find on your way to work (school) or avoid stepping on cracks in the sidewalk?

**2990** WYR narrate everything you do or carry your partner on your back?

**2991** WYR have a stranger stand too close to you in an elevator or stand still for four hours as a living statue?

**2992** WYR have a permanent milk mustache or permanently have cookie crumbs in your bed?

**2993** WYR feel compelled to gargle with mouthwash every fifteen minutes or to knock over building block towers stacked by children?

**2994** WYR move your head like a chicken when you walk or have permanently slippery soles on your shoes?

**2995** WYR sweat vinaigrette or cry lemon juice?

**2996** WYR have a chocolate river or a taffy apple tree in your garden?

**2997** WYR grow a tail or an extra leg?

**2998** WYR be able to teleport or own a clone of yourself?

**2999** WYR marry for love or money?

**3000** WYR be all-knowing or have your life filled with materialistic things?

## About Us

We're an odd bunch of fun, quirky, and creative authors who love writing thought-provoking questions. And we're on a mission to spark engaging discussions.

We've all experienced awkward silence situations and resorted to superficial chitchat and small talk to pass time.

The authors here at *Questions About Me* are on a mission to end dull conversations. We created the *Questions About Me* series to invigorate conversations and help you get to know people better – including yourself.

Put down your phone, switch off the TV, and use our *Questions About Me* books to unlock endless conversational possibilities, provide an abundance of fun memories, and develop deeper relationships.

**www.questionsaboutme.com**

## Also by Questions About Me

3000 Unique Questions About Me

2000 Unique Questions About Me

1000 Unique Questions About Me

Made in United States
Troutdale, OR
11/09/2023

14421134R00099